Okay-okay! We know you're eager to start but first please let u

HOW TO USE THIS BOOK

This book is divided into 4 sections:

1. Hangul Crash Course

If you are completely new to Korean writing this section will jump-start your learning process. Start with the basics and gradually move on to more sophisticated stuff.

2. Syllable Writing Practice

Hangul syllables are not meant to be learned by heart. However, you would have it easier with reading and writing in Korean after you've practiced those syllables a couple hundred times. Cut and copy pages from this workbook to have additional training materials.

3. Words Writing Practice

Writing Hangul syllables is fun but writing real words and phrases in Korean is even more so. In this section we've collected over 200 words and useful phrases for you to practice.

4. Hangul Flash Cards

Print out these pages and cut them along the cross lines. There you'll have your own flash cards with a Hangul letter on one side and its name and romanized reading on the other. No need to spend extra on buying those fancy cardboard cards!

WARNING! This book uses standard romanization of Hangul characters (representing Korean language in Latin letters) to ease your start in understanding the Korean writing system. However, we strongly advise you not to use romanization as a way to understand how these symbols are actually pronounced. A lot of Korean characters have no direct equivalent in English so that the romanization can be misleading. Please refer to audio courses that are available online to get an idea of proper pronunciation (even Google Translate will do).

Let's not hold you up any further!

공부하자!

(Gongbuhaja! - Let's study!)

We are happily accepting feedback regarding this workbook at:
lilas.publishing@ya.ru

Lilas Lingvo Team

Contents

한글 크래시 코스

Hangul Crash Course

1

Hangul Chart

ㄱ	ㄴ	ㄷ	ㅈ	ㅁ	ㅂ	ㅅ
[g/-k]	[n]	[d/-t]	[j]	[m]	[b/-p]	[s]
ㅋ	ㅇ	ㅌ	ㅊ	ㄹ	ㅍ	ㅎ
[k]	[-/-ng]	[t]	[ch]	[r/-l]	[p]	[h]

Vowels

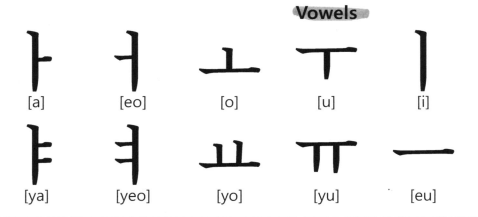

ㅏ	ㅓ	ㅗ	ㅜ	ㅣ
[a]	[eo]	[o]	[u]	[i]
ㅑ	ㅕ	ㅛ	ㅠ	ㅡ
[ya]	[yeo]	[yo]	[yu]	[eu]

Vowel combinations

ㅐ	ㅔ	ㅒ	ㅖ
[ae]	[e]	[yae]	[ye]

Dipthongs

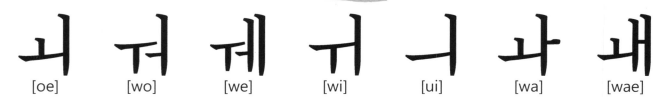

ㅚ	ㅝ	ㅞ	ㅟ	ㅢ	ㅘ	ㅙ
[oe]	[wo]	[we]	[wi]	[ui]	[wa]	[wae]

Double consonants

ㄲ	ㄸ	ㅃ	ㅉ	ㅆ
[gg/-kk]	[dd/-tt]	[bb/-pp]	[jj]	[ss]

Syllabic Blocks

Korean writing system (called Hangul) might seem very complicated at first glance. However unlike other Asian writing systems like Chinese and Japanese Hangul is rather easy to learn because it is actually an alphabet. We don't need to memorize hundreds of symbols but only 24 unique letters: 14 consonants and 10 vowels. There are other symbols but they're merely combinations of the basic ones (see the chart on the left).

The seeming complexity of Hangul comes from the fact that words are not written with individual letters but rather with syllabic blocks that combine several letters together.

For example the word "Hangul" is not written like that: ㅎ ㅏ ㄴ ㄱ ㅡ ㄹ

but rather like that: 한글

There're thousands of variations of syllabic blocks but let us repeat once again - we don't need to memorize them. We only need to remember 24 basic letters to be able to read and write.

In order to write a Hangul syllable we need at least 2 letters: one consonant and one vowel. Let's learn our first letters and practice writing them! Please mind the stroke order as shown by the arrows!

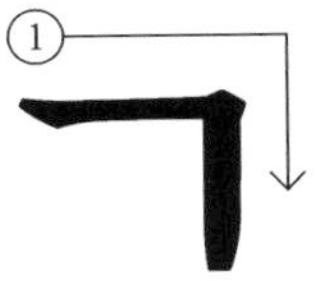

Type: **consonant**
Pronunciation: **[g/-k]**

� Tip: this consonant sounds similar to the English "G" and looks like a Gun.

기역 [gi-yeok]

Practice writing this letter:

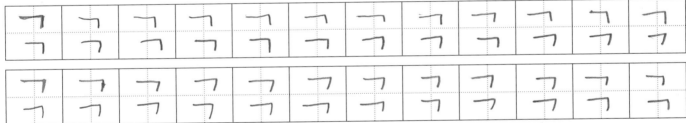

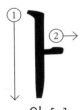

Type: **vowel**
Pronunciation: **[a]**

아 [a]

Practice writing this letter:

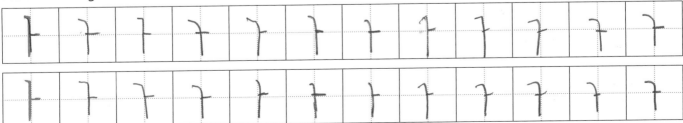

Vertical syllable block

Now that we know our first vowel and consonant let's write our very first Hangul syllable. To do this we need to get acquainted with our first syllable block type that combines a consonant and a vowel side-by-side.

C - consonant
V - vowel

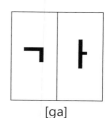

[ga]

If we combine our first consonant ㄱ [g,-k] with our first vowel ㅏ [a] we will get our first syllable: 가 [ga].

Let's practice writing that syllable! Notice how the vertical stroke of the letter ㄱ bends to better fill its allocated space in the syllable block. Please also pay attention to stroke order!

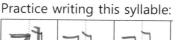
Practice writing this syllable:

[ga]

Now that we know how to write Hangul syllables let's learn some more consonants to combine with our first vowel ㅏ [a]!

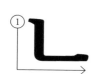

Type: **consonant**
Pronunciation: **[n]**

Tip: this consonant sounds similar to the English "N" and looks like a North-East section of a compass.

ㄴ은 [ni-eun]

Practice writing this letter:

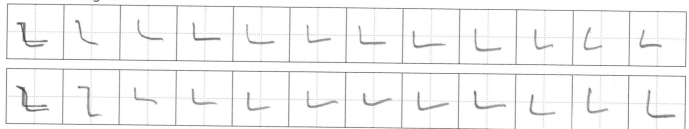

Let's combine our new consonant ㄴ [n] with the vowel ㅏ [a] that we already know:

Practice writing this syllable:

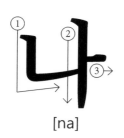

[na]

4

Type: **consonant**
Pronunciation: **[d/-t]**

☀ Tip: this consonant sounds similar to the English "D" and looks like a <u>D</u>oor.

디귿 [di-geut]

Practice writing this letter:

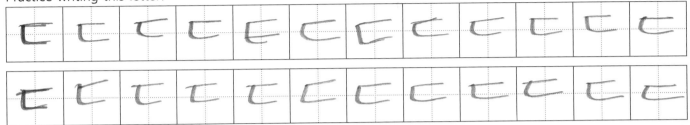

Let's combine consonant ㄷ [d,-t] with the vowel ㅏ [a]:

Practice writing this syllable:

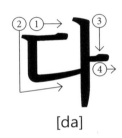

[da]

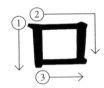

Type: **consonant**
Pronunciation: **[m]**

☀ Tip: this consonant sounds similar to the English "M" and looks like a <u>M</u>ail envelope.

미음 [mi-eum]

Practice writing this letter:

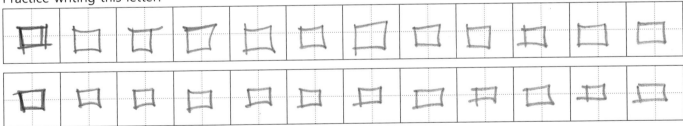

Let's combine consonant ㅁ [m] with the vowel ㅏ [a]:

Practice writing this syllable:

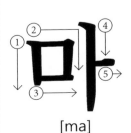

[ma]

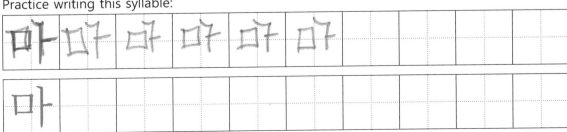

5

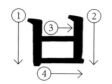

Type: consonant
Pronunciation: [b/-p]

Tip: this consonant sounds similar to the English "B" and looks like a Bed.

비읍 [bi-eup]

Practice writing this letter:

Let's combine consonant ㅂ [b,-p] with the vowel ㅏ [a]:

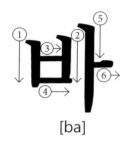

Practice writing this syllable yourself:

[ba]

Type: consonant
Pronunciation: [s]

Tip: this consonant sounds similar to the English "S" and looks like an open Seashell.

시옷 [shi-ot]

Practice writing this letter:

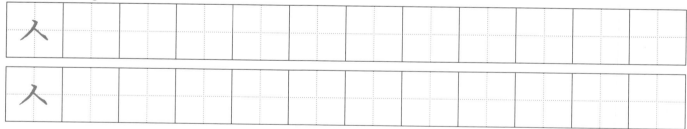

Let's combine consonant ㅅ [s] with the vowel ㅏ [a]:

Practice writing this syllable:

[sa]

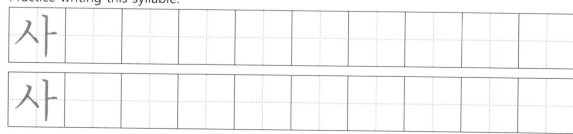

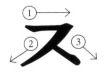

Type: **consonant**
Pronunciation: **[j]**

Tip: this consonant sounds similar to the English "J" and looks somewhat like a Jug.

지읒 [ji-eut]

Practice writing this letter:

ㅈ									
ㅈ									

Let's combine consonant ㅈ [j] with the vowel ㅏ [a]:

Practice writing this syllable:

자									
자									

[ja]

Type: **consonant**
Pronunciation: **[h]**

Tip: this consonant sounds similar to the English "H" and looks like a Hat.

히읗 [hi-eut]

Practice writing this letter:

ㅎ									
ㅎ									

Let's combine consonant ㅎ [h] with the vowel ㅏ [a]:

Practice writing this syllable:

하									
하									

[ha]

7

Now let's learn our second vowel:

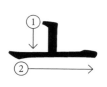

Type: **vowel**
Pronunciation: **[o]**

오 [o]

Practice writing this letter:

ㅗ													

ㅗ													

Horizontal syllable block

Our first vowel ㅏ [a] was <u>vertical</u> thus we used it in a vertical syllable block. Vowel ㅗ [o] however is <u>horizontal</u> thus we need to use a horizontal syllable block.

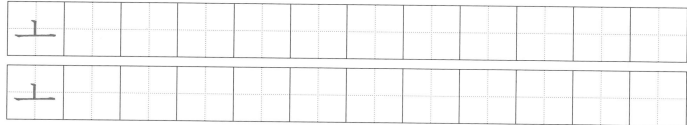

C - consonant
V - vowel

Let's try combining all of the consonants that we've learned so far with our new vowel ㅗ [o].

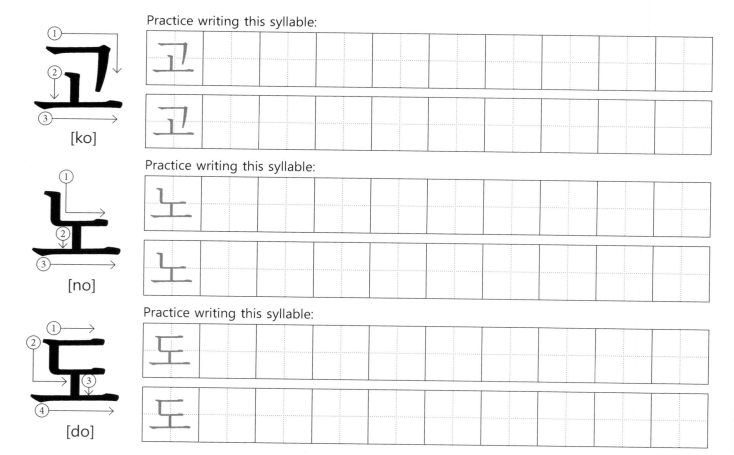

Practice writing this syllable:

[ko]

Practice writing this syllable:

[no]

Practice writing this syllable:

[do]

Practice writing this syllable:

모
[mo]

Practice writing this syllable:

보
[bo]

Practice writing this syllable:

소
[so]

Practice writing this syllable:

조
[jo]

Practice writing this syllable:

호
[ho]

And once again with both vowels ㅏ [a] and ㅗ [o]:

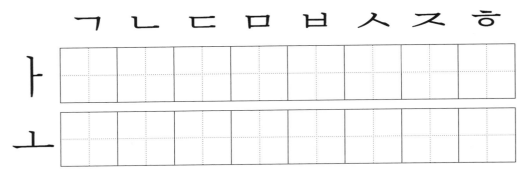

ㄱ ㄴ ㄷ ㅁ ㅂ ㅅ ㅈ ㅎ

ㅏ

ㅗ

Now let's learn another consonant:

 Type: **consonant**
Pronunciation: **[r/-l]**

☀ Tip: this consonant sounds similar to the English "L" and looks like a Ladder.

리을 [ri-eul/li-eul]

Practice writing this letter:

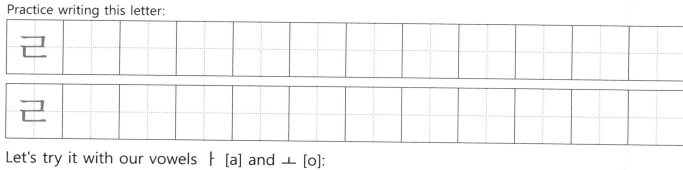

Let's try it with our vowels ㅏ [a] and ㅗ [o]:

Practice writing this syllable:

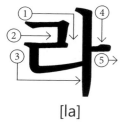
[la]

Practice writing this syllable:

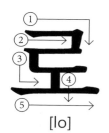
[lo]

And on to our next consonant which is a rather special one:

 Type: **consonant**
Pronunciation: **[-/-ng]**

☀ Tip: this consonant when used in front of a vowel has zero sound and it looks like a zero.

이응 [i-eung]

Practice writing this letter yourself:

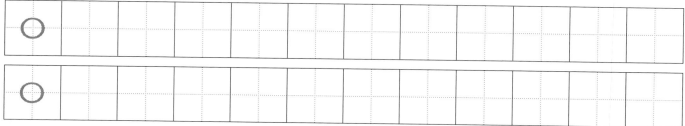

Empty sound consonant

Up till now we have only used syllables that start with a consonant. But how do we make a vowel sound without a consonant? To do that we would use letter ㅇ. When it is placed at the beginning of a syllable it has no sound and thus it allows the vowel to sound on its own. This would be the first use for letter ㅇ. Let's try using letter ㅇ with vowels ㅏ [a] and ㅗ [o] that we already know.

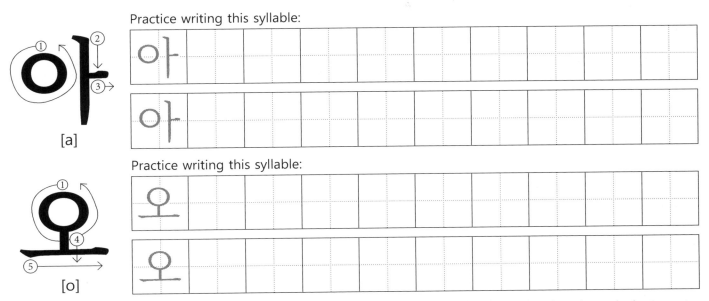

Practice writing this syllable:

아

아

[a]

Practice writing this syllable:

오

오

[o]

💡 In words that contain ㅇ letter as an empty sound syllables can blend with each other through that empty sound when pronounced. For example the word 한국인 which means "a Korean person" reads [hangugin] not [han-gug-in].

Three-letter syllables

The second use for the letter ㅇ is to be put at the end of a syllable. But in order to do that we first need to learn two new types of syllable blocks that contain an ending consonant:

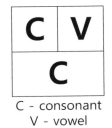

C - consonant
V - vowel

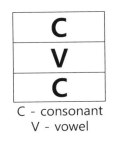

C - consonant
V - vowel

Using these new syllabic block types you can combine 2 consonants and 1 vowel into one syllable. The block to the left is used with vertical vowels and the block to the right - with horizontal vowels.

Let's practice writing these new syllable blocks with vowels and consonants that we already know!

Practice writing this syllable. Use the stroke order instructions from the previous pages:

간

간

[gan]

Practice writing these syllables. Use the stroke order instructions from the previous pages:

녹
[nog]

달
[dal]

랍
[lab]

목
[mog]

볼
[bol]

산
[san]

접
[jeob]

녹											
녹											
달											
달											
랍											
랍											
목											
목											
볼											
볼											
산											
산											
접											
접											

Letter ㅇ at the end of the syllable

The second use for consonant ㅇ is as we've already mentioned above to be placed at the end of a syllable block. In that position it produces an [-ng] sound.

Let's try using the letter ㅇ this way!

Practice writing these syllables. Use the stroke order instructions from the previous pages:

공 [gong]

낭 [nang]

동 [dong]

랑 [lang]

몽 [mong]

장 [jang]

Let's practice everything that we've learned so far!

Practice writing these syllables. Use the stroke order instructions from the previous pages:

아
[a]

고
[go]

앙
[ang]

옹
[ong]

람
[lam]

졸
[jol]

삽
[sab]

Practice writing these syllables. Use the stroke order instructions from the previous pages:

오 [o]

바 [ba]

잘 [jal]

압 [ab]

롱 [long]

족 [jog]

손 [son]

Vowels ㅓ, ㅜ, ㅣ and ㅡ

Now that we've learned quite a lot of consonants let's expand our range of vowels as well!

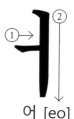

어 [eo]

Type: **vowel**
Pronunciation: **[eo]**

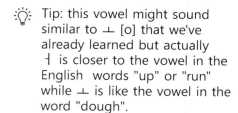
Tip: this vowel might sound similar to ㅗ [o] that we've already learned but actually ㅓ is closer to the vowel in the English words "up" or "run" while ㅗ is like the vowel in the word "dough".

Practice writing this letter:

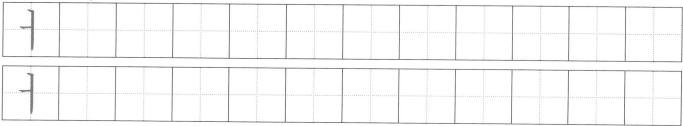

Type: **vowel**
Pronunciation: **[u]**

우 [u]

Practice writing this letter:

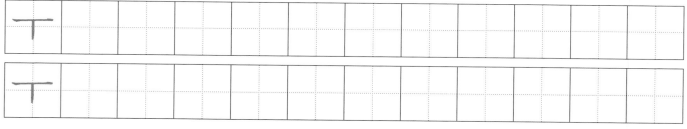

Type: **vowel**
Pronunciation: **[eu]**

Tip: this vowel sound similar to [u] in the word "brook" and looks like a stream.

으 [eu]

Practice writing this letter:

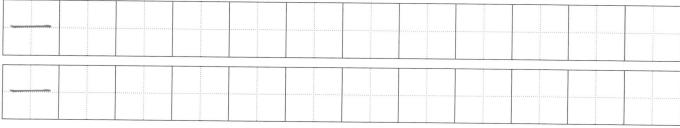

이 [i]

Type: **vowel**
Pronunciation: **[i]**

Tip: this vowel sound similar to [i] in the word "tree" and looks like a trunk of a tree.

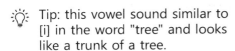

Practice writing this letter:

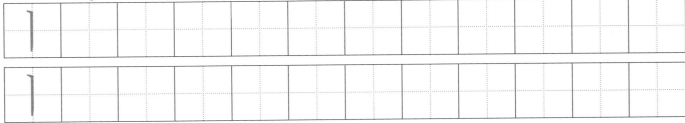

Tip: use the phrase "There's no t<u>ree</u> without a br<u>oo</u>k." to remember vowels ㅣ and ㅡ.

Tip: when ㅣ [i] is combined with the consonant ㅅ [s] the resulting sound is [shi] not [si].

Now let's put everything we've learned so far together and practice!

Practice writing these syllables. Use the stroke order instructions from the previous pages:

고
[ko]

거
[geo]

도
[do]

너
[neo]

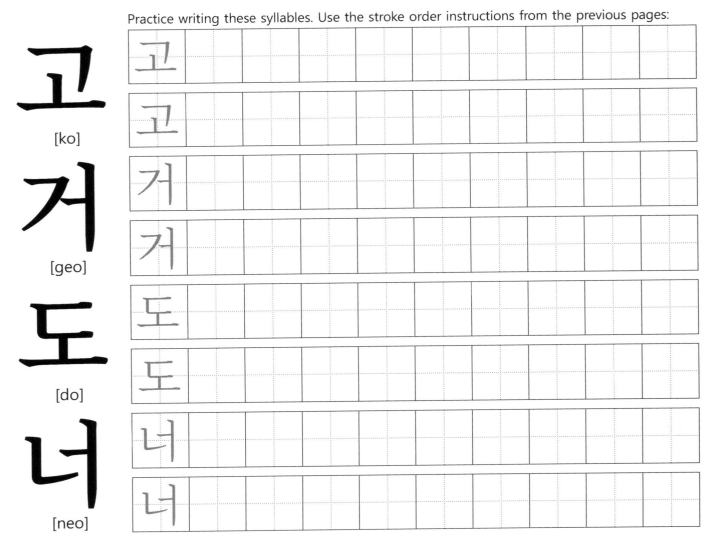

Practice writing these syllables. Use the stroke order instructions from the previous pages:

놀
[nol]

런
[leon]

우
[u]

군
[gun]

물
[mul]

브
[beu]

즈
[jeu]

Practice writing these syllables. Use the stroke order instructions from the previous pages:

흔 [heun]

빌 [bil]

밈 [mim]

선 [seon]

눈 [nun]

실 [shil]

심 [shim]

19

Vowels ㅔ, ㅐ, ㅑ and ㅛ

Let's learn some more vowels!

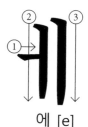

에 [e]

Type: **vowel**
Pronunciation: **[e]**

Practice writing this letter:

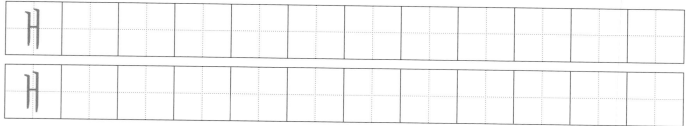

Type: **vowel**
Pronunciation: **[ae]**

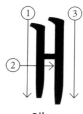

애 [ae]

💡 Tip: vowel ㅔ (above) and vowel ㅐ sound exactly the same - like the [e] sound in the word "Egg".

Practice writing this letter:

Type: **vowel**
Pronunciation: **[ya]**

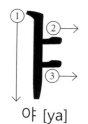

야 [ya]

💡 Tip: vowel ㅑ [ya] is a combination of vowels ㅣ [i] and ㅏ [a]

Practice writing this letter:

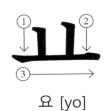

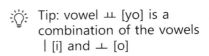
Tip: vowel ㅛ [yo] is a combination of the vowels ㅣ [i] and ㅗ [o]

Type: **vowel**
Pronunciation: **[yo]**

요 [yo]

Practice writing this letter:

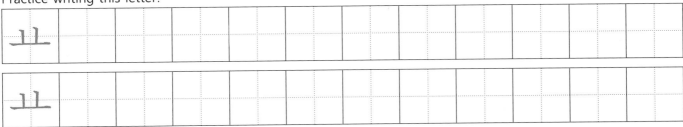

Tip: when ㅑ [ya] and ㅛ [yo] are combined with the consonant ㅅ [s] the resulting sounds are 샤 [shya] and 쇼 [shyo] starting with [sh].

Now let's put everything we've learned so far together and practice!

Practice writing these syllables. Use the stroke order instructions from the previous pages:

게
[ge]

래
[lae]

샥
[shyag]

교
[gyo]

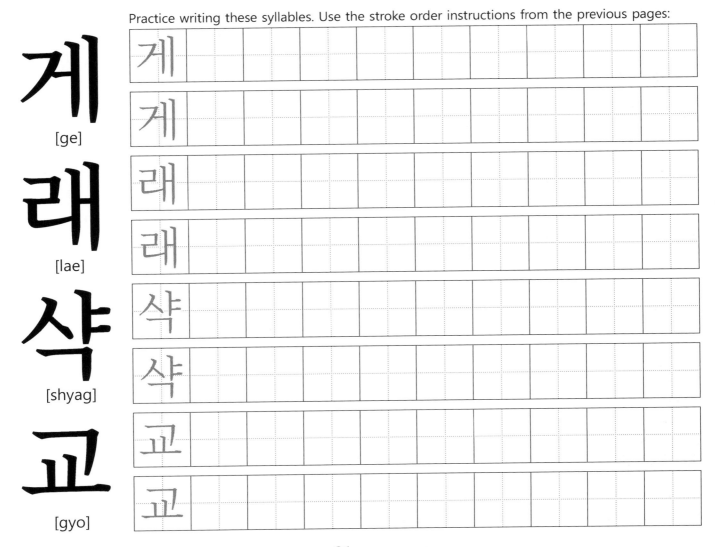

21

행 [haeng]

낙 [nyag]

욕 [yog]

베 [be]

세 [se]

묘 [myo]

졀 [jyeol]

Practice writing these syllables. Use the stroke order instructions from the previous pages:

행								
행								
냑								
냑								
욕								
욕								
베								
베								
세								
세								
묘								
묘								
졀								
졀								

Practice writing these syllables. Use the stroke order instructions from the previous pages:

매
[mae]

효
[hyo]

갸
[gya]

녑
[nyeob]

게
[ge]

쟈
[jya]

뇨
[nyo]

Vowels ㅕ, ㅠ, ㅖ and ㅒ

And finally the last set of four vowels that we need to learn!

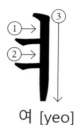

여 [yeo]

Type: vowel
Pronunciation: [yeo]

💡 Tip: this vowel is a combination of the vowels ㅣ [i] and ㅓ [eo].

Practice writing this letter:

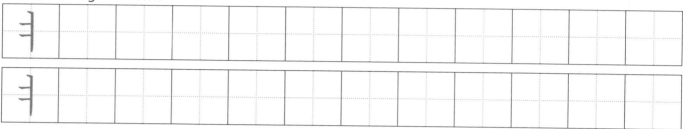

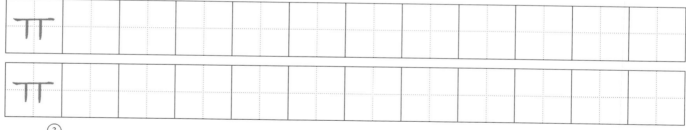

유 [yu]

Type: vowel
Pronunciation: [yu]

💡 Tip: this vowel is a combination of vowels ㅣ [i] and ㅜ [u].

Practice writing this letter:

예 [ye]

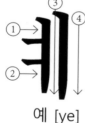

Type: vowel
Pronunciation: [ye]

💡 Tip: this vowel is a combination of the vowels ㅣ [i] and ㅔ [e].

Practice writing this letter:

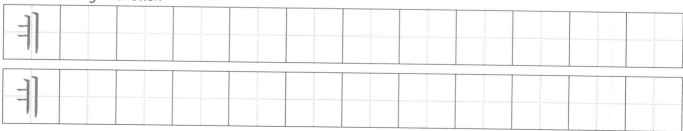

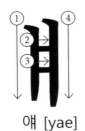

애 [yae]

Type: **vowel**
Pronunciation: **[yae]**

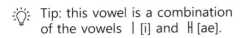
Practice writing this letter:

ㅒ

ㅒ

Tip: vowels ㅖ [ye] and ㅒ [yae] are pronounced the same way.

Now once again let's put everything we've learned so far together and practice!

Practice writing these syllables. Use the stroke order instructions from the previous pages:

여
[yeo]

여

여

유
[yu]

유

유

예
[ye]

예

예

애
[yae]

얘

얘

역
[yeog]

윤
[yun]

계
[gye]

내
[nyae]

혀
[hyeo]

뷰
[byu]

옙
[yeb]

Practice writing these syllables. Use the stroke order instructions from the previous pages:

역

역

윤

윤

계

계

내

내

혀

혀

뷰

뷰

옙

옙

얨
[yaem]

져
[jye]

얠
[yael]

뮥
[myug]

헨
[hyed]

셤
[syeom]

육
[yug]

Four-letter syllable blocks

Now that we've learned all the Hangul vowels let's get acquainted with two new syllable blocks!

C	V
C	C

For use with vertical vowels.

C - consonant
V - vowel

C
V
C C

For use with horizontal vowels.

C - consonant
V - vowel

If a 4-letter syllable is followed by a syllable with an empty sound the last consonant of the 4-letter syllable blends with the next syllable like in this example:

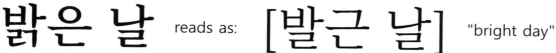

밝은 날   reads as: [발근 날]   "bright day"

[balgeun nal]

A lot of times 4-letter syllables are composed with consonant ㄹ [r/-l] at the bottom. In most of these cases the ㄹ consonant will not be pronounced. For example:

1. 삶 reads as: [삼]   2. 흙 reads as: [흑]

[salm]   [heug]

A notable exception from this rule is:

여덟 which reads as: [여달] "eight"

[yeodeolb]

Practice writing these 4-letter syllables:

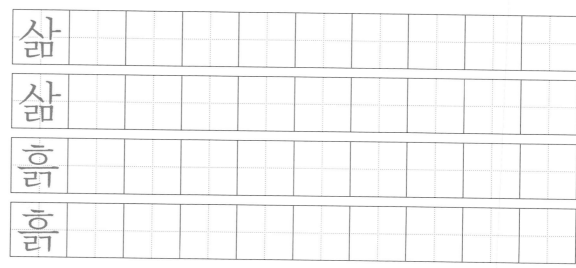

삶
[sam]

흙
[heug]

삶 삶

흙 흙

28

Double consonants

The next set of Hangul letters that we need to learn are double consonants.

💡 Tip: please refer to any Korean audio course available to you to get the pronunciation of double consonants right.

 Type: **double consonant**
Pronunciation: **[gg/-kk]**

💡 Tip: double consonants are easy to learn as they are just two basic consonants written together.

The stroke order is also the same as for the basic ones.

쌍기역 [ssang-giyeok]

Practice writing this letter:

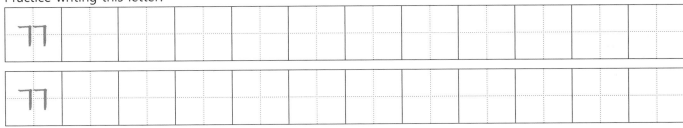

 Type: **double consonant**
Pronunciation: **[dd/-tt]**

쌍디귿 [ssang-digeut]

Practice writing this letter:

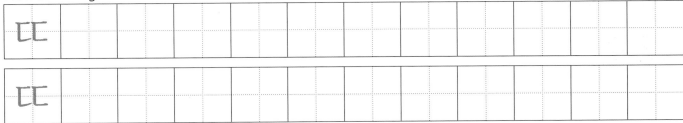

 Type: **double consonant**
Pronunciation: **[bb/-pp]**

쌍비읍 [ssang-bi-eup]

Practice writing this letter:

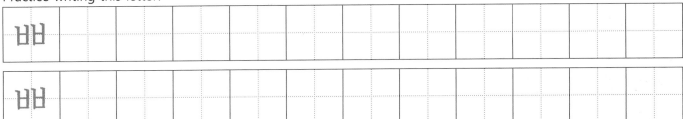

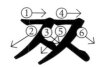

Type: **double consonant**
Pronunciation: **[jj]**

쌍지읒 [ssang-ji-eut]

Practice writing this letter:

짜

짜

Type: **double consonant**
Pronunciation: **[ss]**

쌍시옷 [ssang-si-ot]

Practice writing this letter:

쓰

쓰

Let's practice writing syllables with double consonants:

Practice writing these syllables. Use the stroke order instructions from the previous pages:

꼼
[kkom]

꼼

꼼

땅
[ttang]

땅

땅

삥
[pping]

삥

삥

쓸
[sseul]

찜
[jjim]

뽀
[ppo]

씨
[ssi]

뜸
[tteum]

쩐
[jjeon]

끈
[kkeun]

Practice writing these syllables. Use the stroke order instructions from the previous pages:

쓸

쓸

찜

찜

뽀

뽀

씨

씨

뜸

뜸

쩐

쩐

끈

끈

Practice writing these syllables yourself. Use stroke order instructions from the previous pages:

띠
[tti]

써
[sseo]

빠
[ppya]

쭈
[jju]

꼬
[kko]

쌈
[ssam]

쁜
[ppeun]

Strong consonants

The next set of letters that we need to learn are strong consonants.

💡 Tip: strong consonants are pronounced almost the same way as the regular ones but stronger.

Type: **strong consonant**
Pronunciation: **[k]**

💡 Tip: strong consonant ㅋ is a stronger version of regular consonant ㄱ.

💡 Tip: consonant ㅋ sounds like English [k] and looks like a <u>K</u>ey.

키읔 [ki-euk]

Practice writing this letter:

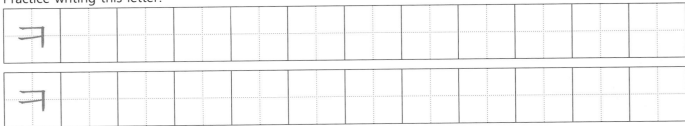

Type: **strong consonant**
Pronunciation: **[t]**

💡 Tip: strong consonant ㅌ is a stronger version of regular consonant ㄷ.

💡 Tip: consonant ㅌ sounds like English [t] and looks like <u>T</u>eeth of a pitchfork.

티읕 [ti-eut]

Practice writing this letter:

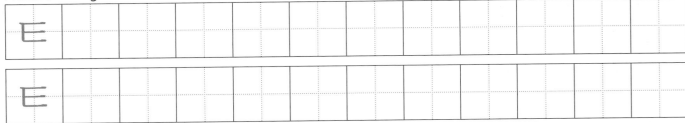

Type: **strong consonant**
Pronunciation: **[p]**

💡 Tip: strong consonant ㅍ is a stronger version of regular consonant ㅂ.

💡 Tip: consonant ㅍ sounds like English [p] and looks like letter **π** [pi].

피읖 [pi-eup]

Practice writing this letter:

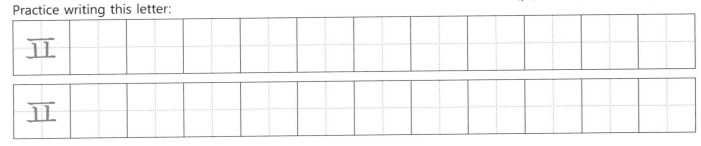

Type: **strong consonant**
Pronunciation: **[ch]**

💡 Tip: strong consonant ㅊ is a stronger version of regular consonant ㅈ.

💡 Tip: consonant ㅊ sounds like [ch] and looks like a <u>Ch</u>urch.

치읓 [chi-eut]

Practice writing this letter:

ㅊ

ㅊ

Now let's practice writing syllables with regular, double and strong consonants:

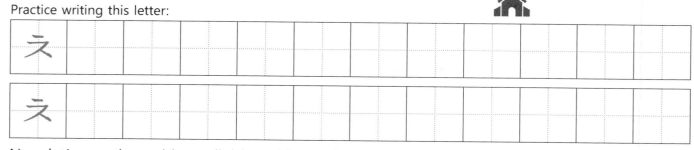

Practice writing these syllables. Use the stroke order instructions from the previous pages:

가
[ga]

까
[kka]

카
[ka]

도
[do]

또
[tto]

Practice writing these syllables. Use the stroke order instructions from the previous pages:

토 [to]

비 [bi]

삐 [ppi]

피 [pi]

즈 [jeu]

쯔 [jjeu]

츠 [cheu]

Practice writing these syllables. Use the stroke order instructions from the previous pages:

굼
[gum]

꿈
[kkum]

쿰
[kum]

반
[ban]

빤
[ppan]

판
[pan]

즐
[jeul]

쫄
[jjeul]

츨
[cheul]

Diphthongs

Dipthongs are vowels but fortunately there is no need to learn anything new. These are combinations of vowels that we already know!

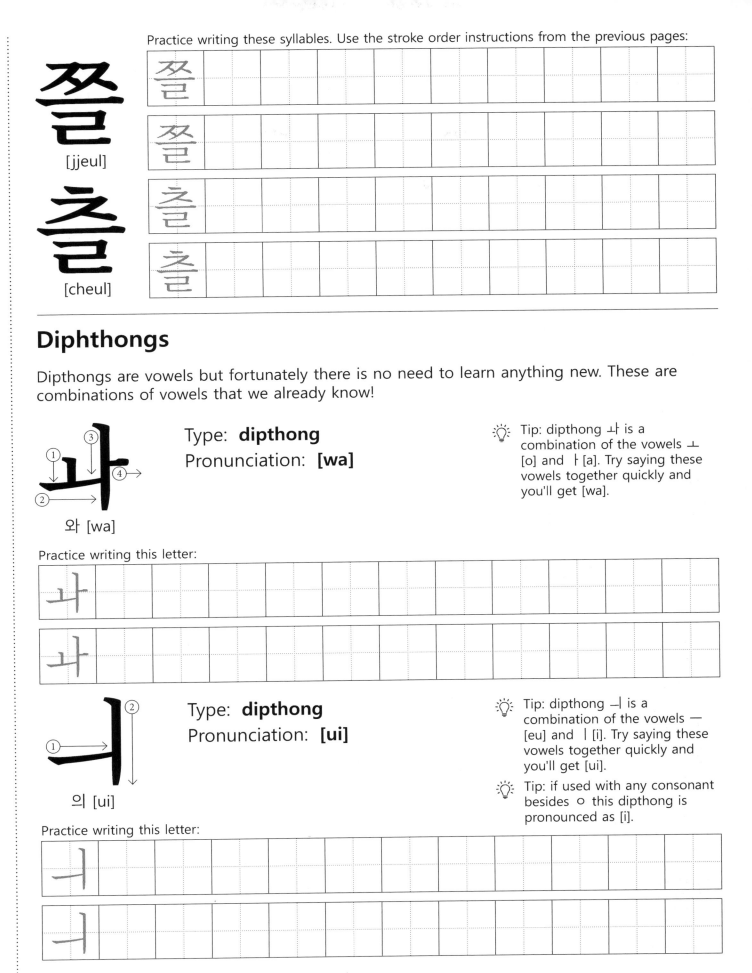

와 [wa]

Type: **dipthong**

Pronunciation: **[wa]**

Tip: dipthong ㅘ is a combination of the vowels ㅗ [o] and ㅏ [a]. Try saying these vowels together quickly and you'll get [wa].

Practice writing this letter:

의 [ui]

Type: **dipthong**

Pronunciation: **[ui]**

Tip: dipthong ㅢ is a combination of the vowels ㅡ [eu] and ㅣ [i]. Try saying these vowels together quickly and you'll get [ui].

Tip: if used with any consonant besides ㅇ this dipthong is pronounced as [i].

Practice writing this letter:

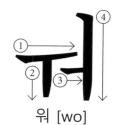

워 [wo]

Type: **dipthong**
Pronunciation: **[wo]**

Tip: dipthong ㅝ is a combination of the vowels ㅜ [u] and ㅓ [eu]. Try saying these vowels together quickly and you'll get [wo].

Practice writing this letter:

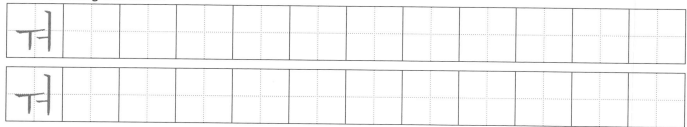

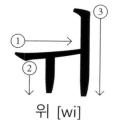

위 [wi]

Type: **dipthong**
Pronunciation: **[wi]**

Tip: dipthong ㅟ is a combination of the vowels ㅜ [u] and ㅣ [i]. Try saying these vowels together quickly and you'll get [wi].

Practice writing this letter:

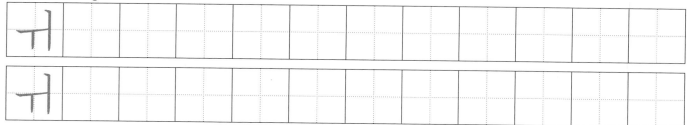

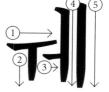

웨 [we]

Type: **dipthong**
Pronunciation: **[we]**

Tip: dipthong ㅞ is a combination of vowels ㅜ [u] and ㅔ [e]. Try saying these vowels together quickly and you'll get [we].

Practice writing this letter yourself:

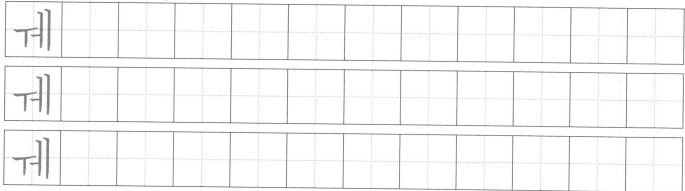

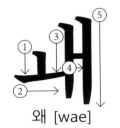

Type: dipthong

Pronunciation: **[wae]**

💡 Tip: dipthong ㅙ is a combination of the vowels ㅗ [o] and ㅐ [ae]. Try saying these vowels together quickly and you'll get [wae].

왜 [wae]

Practice writing this letter:

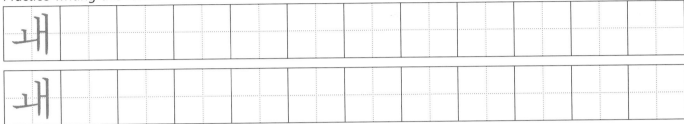

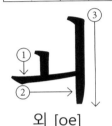

Type: dipthong

Pronunciation: **[oe]**

💡 Tip: dipthong ㅚ looks like a combination of vowels ㅗ [o] and ㅣ [i] but actually it is a combination of ㅗ [o] and ㅔ [e] and sounds as [oe]

💡 Tip: dipthong ㅚ [oe] and dipthong ㅙ [wae] basically sound the same way.

외 [oe]

Practice writing this letter:

Now let's practice writing syllables with dipthongs:

Practice writing these syllables. Use the stroke order instructions from the previous pages:

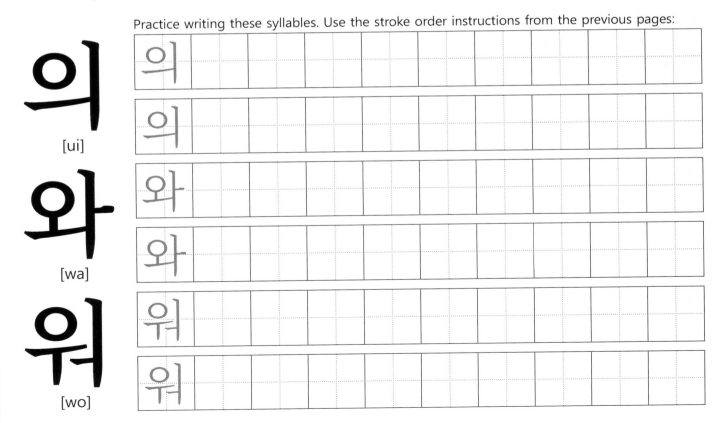

의
[ui]

와
[wa]

워
[wo]

Practice writing these syllables. Use the stroke order instructions from the previous pages:

위
[wi]

왜
[wae]

외
[oe]

웨
[we]

싀
[sui]

봐
[bwa]

뒈
[dwo]

Practice writing these syllables. Use the stroke order instructions from the previous pages:

뉘
[nwi]

괘
[gwae]

괴
[goe]

궤
[gwe]

흰
[huin]

관
[gwan]

궝
[gwong]

Practice writing these syllables. Use the stroke order instructions from the previous pages:

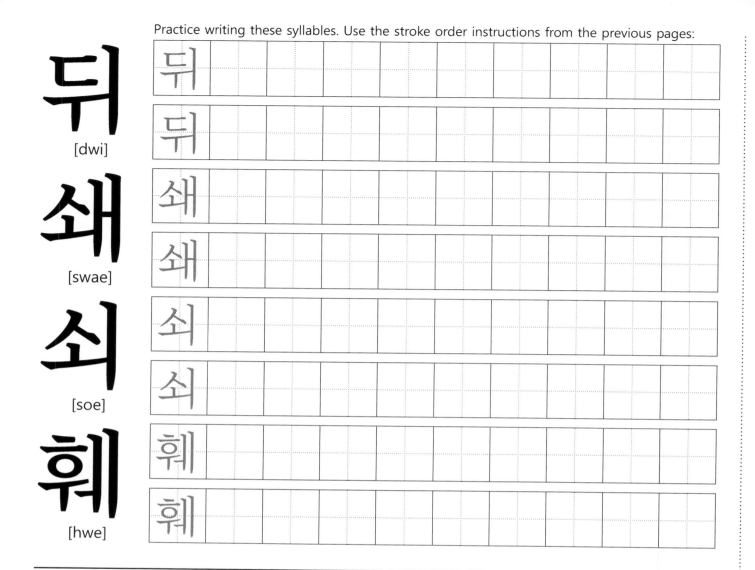

뒤
[dwi]

쇄
[swae]

쇠
[soe]

훼
[hwe]

Congratulations! You have now learned all the consonants and vowels of Hangul!

축하합니다!

"Congratulations!"

Sound changing rules

Before we finish our Hangul crash course let's learn some Korean sound changing rules so that you would not be confused when confronted with certain letter combinations.

1. Re-syllabification

When a final consonant meets a starting vowel, the consonant carries over.
Ending ㅇ (ng) does not carry over. Ending ㅎ is dropped.

Examples:

십오 reads as [시보], 한국어 reads as [한구거], 좋아 reads as [조아]

2. Ending consonant simplification

Ending consonants ㅋ, ㄲ are pronounced as ㄱ.
Ending consonants ㅅ, ㅈ, ㅊ, ㅌ, ㅎ, ㅆ are pronounced as ㄷ (except when followed by ㅇ).
Ending consonant ㅍ is pronounced as ㅂ.

Examples:

구억 reads as [구억], 끝 reads as [끋], 맛 reads as [맏], 꽃 reads as [꼳]
앞 reads as [압], 맛이 reads as [마시] (exception)

3. Reinforcement/intensification

Ending consonants ㄱ,ㅂ,ㅈ,ㄷ change the starting consonant of the next character to a double consonant.
Ending consonant ㅎ only changes starting consonant ㅅ to ㅆ.

Examples:

학교 reads as [학꾜], 학생 reads as [학쌩], 잡지 reads as [잡찌],
먹다 reads as [먹따], 좋습니다 reads as [조씁니다]

4. Nasalization

When ending consonants meet nasal sounds (ㅁ,ㄴ) they will change:
ㄱ to ㅇ; ㄷ/ㅅ/ㅈ to ㄴ; ㅂ to ㅁ
Exception: when consonant ㄱ meets a starting consonant ㄹ they change:
ㄱ to ㅇ and ㄹ to ㄴ.

Examples:

국내 reads as [궁내], 맞는 reads as [만는], 업무 reads as [엄무]
합니다 reads as [함니다], 독립 reads as [동닙]

5. Assimilation

When ending consonant ㄹ meets starting consonant ㄴ or vise versa both consonants are pronounced as ㄹ.

Examples:

실내 reads as [실래]
신라 reads as [실라]

6. Aspiration

When consonants ㄱ, ㄷ, ㅂ, ㅈ meet ㅎ they will strengthen / aspirate into ㅋ, ㅌ, ㅍ, ㅊ
Exception: when consonant ㅅ meets consonant ㅎ it may change to ㅌ.

Examples:

북한 reads as [부칸]
좋다 reads as [조타]
급행 reads as [그팽]
맞히다 reads as [마치다]
못하다 reads as [모타다]

7. Palatization

When ending consonant ㄷ meets 이 it is pronounced as 지.
When ending consonant ㅌ meets 이 it is pronounced as 치

Examples:

굳이 reads as [구지]
같이 reads as [가치]

8. Intrusive ㄴ

If in a compound word ending consonant meets starting vowel 이/여/야/유/요, add starting ㄴ.

Examples:

꽃+잎 turns to: [꽃+닢] and finally reads as: [꼰닙]

음절 쓰기 연습

Syllable Writing Practice

Basic syllable chart (기본 음절)

	ㅏ	ㅑ	ㅓ	ㅕ	ㅗ	ㅛ	ㅜ	ㅠ	ㅡ	ㅣ
ㄱ	가	갸	거	겨	고	교	구	규	그	기
ㄴ	나	냐	너	녀	노	뇨	누	뉴	느	니
ㄷ	다	댜	더	뎌	도	됴	두	듀	드	디
ㄹ	라	랴	러	려	로	료	루	류	르	리
ㅁ	마	먀	머	며	모	묘	무	뮤	므	미
ㅂ	바	뱌	버	벼	보	뵤	부	뷰	브	비
ㅅ	사	샤	서	셔	소	쇼	수	슈	스	시
ㅇ	아	야	어	여	오	요	우	유	으	이
ㅈ	자	쟈	저	져	조	죠	주	쥬	즈	지
ㅊ	차	챠	처	쳐	초	쵸	추	츄	츠	치
ㅋ	카	캬	커	켜	코	쿄	쿠	큐	크	키
ㅌ	타	탸	터	텨	토	툐	투	튜	트	티
ㅍ	파	퍄	퍼	펴	포	표	푸	퓨	프	피
ㅎ	하	햐	허	혀	호	효	후	휴	흐	히

Consonants + ㅏ

가 | 가 가 가
나 | 나 나 나
다 | 다 다 다
라 | 라 라 라
마 | 마 마 마
바 | 바 바 바
사 | 사 사 사
아 | 아 아 아
자 | 자 자 자
차 | 차 차 차
카 | 카 카 카
타 | 타 타 타
파 | 파 파 파
하 | 하 하 하

Consonants + ㅏ + ending consonant

강 | 강 강 강
낲 | 낲 낲 낲
닽 | 닽 닽 닽
락 | 락 락 락
맞 | 맞 맞 맞
밫 | 밫 밫 밫
상 | 상 상 상
앗 | 앗 앗 앗
잡 | 잡 잡 잡
참 | 참 참 참
칼 | 칼 칼 칼
탇 | 탇 탇 탇
판 | 판 판 판
학 | 학 학 학

Consonants + ㅑ

Consonants + ㅑ + ending consonant

걍	걍	걍	걍										
냪	냪	냪	냪										
턑	턑	턑	턑										
럌	럌	럌	럌										
맞	맞	맞	맞										
뱇	뱇	뱇	뱇										
샹	샹	샹	샹										
얏	얏	얏	얏										
쟙	쟙	쟙	쟙										
챰	챰	챰	챰										
컄	컄	컄	컄										
턑	턑	턑	턑										
퍈	퍈	퍈	퍈										
햑	햑	햑	햑										

Consonants + ㅓ

거 | 거 거 거 | | | | | | | | | |

너 | 너 너 너 | | | | | | | | | |

더 | 더 더 더 | | | | | | | | | |

러 | 러 러 러 | | | | | | | | | |

머 | 머 머 머 | | | | | | | | | |

버 | 버 버 버 | | | | | | | | | |

서 | 서 서 서 | | | | | | | | | |

어 | 어 어 어 | | | | | | | | | |

저 | 저 저 저 | | | | | | | | | |

처 | 처 처 처 | | | | | | | | | |

커 | 커 커 커 | | | | | | | | | |

터 | 터 터 터 | | | | | | | | | |

퍼 | 퍼 퍼 퍼 | | | | | | | | | |

허 | 허 허 허 | | | | | | | | | |

Consonants + ㅓ + ending consonant

겅 | 겅 겅 겅
넒 | 넒 넒 넒
덭 | 덭 덭 덭
럭 | 럭 럭 럭
멎 | 멎 멎 멎
벗 | 벗 벗 벗
성 | 성 성 성
엇 | 엇 엇 엇
접 | 접 접 접
첨 | 첨 첨 첨
컬 | 컬 컬 컬
텉 | 텉 텉 텉
펀 | 펀 펀 펀
헉 | 헉 헉 헉

Consonants + ㅕ

겨 | 겨 겨 겨

녀 | 녀 녀 녀

뎌 | 뎌 뎌 뎌

려 | 려 려 려

며 | 며 며 며

벼 | 벼 벼 벼

셔 | 셔 셔 셔

여 | 여 여 여

져 | 져 져 져

쳐 | 쳐 쳐 쳐

켜 | 켜 켜 켜

텨 | 텨 텨 텨

펴 | 펴 펴 펴

혀 | 혀 혀 혀

Consonants + ㅕ + ending consonant

곕	곕	곕	곕										
녋	녋	녋	녋										
뎉	뎉	뎉	뎉										
력	력	력	력										
몆	몆	몆	몆										
볏	볏	볏	볏										
셩	셩	셩	셩										
엿	엿	엿	엿										
졉	졉	졉	졉										
쳠	쳠	쳠	쳠										
켤	켤	켤	켤										
텯	텯	텯	텯										
편	편	편	편										
혁	혁	혁	혁										

Consonants +ㅗ

고	고	고	고									
노	노	노	노									
도	도	도	도									
로	로	로	로									
모	모	모	모									
보	보	보	보									
소	소	소	소									
오	오	오	오									
조	조	조	조									
초	초	초	초									
코	코	코	코									
토	토	토	토									
포	포	포	포									
호	호	호	호									

Consonants +ㅗ+ ending consonant

곻 | 곻 | 곻 | 곻 | | | | | | | | |

놐 | 놐 | 놐 | 놐 | | | | | | | | |

돝 | 돝 | 돝 | 돝 | | | | | | | | |

롥 | 롥 | 롥 | 롥 | | | | | | | | |

못 | 못 | 못 | 못 | | | | | | | | |

봊 | 봊 | 봊 | 봊 | | | | | | | | |

송 | 송 | 송 | 송 | | | | | | | | |

옷 | 옷 | 옷 | 옷 | | | | | | | | |

좁 | 좁 | 좁 | 좁 | | | | | | | | |

촘 | 촘 | 촘 | 촘 | | | | | | | | |

콜 | 콜 | 콜 | 콜 | | | | | | | | |

톤 | 톤 | 톤 | 톤 | | | | | | | | |

폰 | 폰 | 폰 | 폰 | | | | | | | | |

혹 | 혹 | 혹 | 혹 | | | | | | | | |

Consonants +ㅛ

교	교	교	교								
뇨	뇨	뇨	뇨								
됴	됴	됴	됴								
료	료	료	료								
묘	묘	묘	묘								
뵤	뵤	뵤	뵤								
쇼	쇼	쇼	쇼								
요	요	요	요								
죠	죠	죠	죠								
쵸	쵸	쵸	쵸								
쿄	쿄	쿄	쿄								
툐	툐	툐	툐								
표	표	표	표								
효	효	효	효								

Consonants +ㅛ+ ending consonant

콩	콩	콩	콩									
뇬	뇬	뇬	뇬									
됴	됴	됴	됴									
룍	룍	룍	룍									
묫	묫	묫	묫									
뷰	뷰	뷰	뷰									
숑	숑	숑	숑									
욧	욧	욧	욧									
쥼	쥼	쥼	쥼									
춈	춈	춈	춈									
쿌	쿌	쿌	쿌									
튠	튠	튠	튠									
퓬	퓬	퓬	퓬									
횩	횩	횩	횩									

Consonants +ㅜ

구
누
두
루
무
부
수
우
주
추
쿠
투
푸
후

구 구 구
누 누 누
두 두 두
루 루 루
무 무 무
부 부 부
수 수 수
우 우 우
주 주 주
추 추 추
쿠 쿠 쿠
투 투 투
푸 푸 푸
후 후 후

Consonants +ㅜ+ ending consonant

궁 궁 궁 궁

눞 눞 눞 눞

듣 듣 듣 듣

룩 룩 룩 룩

뭇 뭇 뭇 뭇

붓 붓 붓 붓

슝 슝 슝 슝

웃 웃 웃 웃

줌 줌 줌 줌

춤 춤 춤 춤

쿨 쿨 쿨 쿨

툰 툰 툰 툰

푼 푼 푼 푼

훅 훅 훅 훅

Consonants +ㅠ

규
뉴
듀
류
뮤
뷰
슈
유
쥬
츄
큐
튜
퓨
휴

규 규 규
뉴 뉴 뉴
듀 듀 듀
류 류 류
뮤 뮤 뮤
뷰 뷰 뷰
슈 슈 슈
유 유 유
쥬 쥬 쥬
츄 츄 츄
큐 큐 큐
튜 튜 튜
퓨 퓨 퓨
휴 휴 휴

Consonants +ㅠ+ ending consonant

쿵 | 쿵 | 쿵 | 쿵 | | | | | | | | | |

높 | 높 | 높 | 높 | | | | | | | | | |

듣 | 듣 | 듣 | 듣 | | | | | | | | | |

륙 | 륙 | 륙 | 륙 | | | | | | | | | |

뭊 | 뭊 | 뭊 | 뭊 | | | | | | | | | |

뷪 | 뷪 | 뷪 | 뷪 | | | | | | | | | |

슝 | 슝 | 슝 | 슝 | | | | | | | | | |

윳 | 윳 | 윳 | 윳 | | | | | | | | | |

쥼 | 쥼 | 쥼 | 쥼 | | | | | | | | | |

츕 | 츕 | 츕 | 츕 | | | | | | | | | |

큘 | 큘 | 큘 | 큘 | | | | | | | | | |

튠 | 튠 | 튠 | 튠 | | | | | | | | | |

퓬 | 퓬 | 퓬 | 퓬 | | | | | | | | | |

휵 | 휵 | 휵 | 휵 | | | | | | | | | |

Consonants + ㅣ

기

니

디

리

미

비

시

이

지

치

키

티

피

히

Consonants + ㅣ + ending consonant

킹	킹	킹	킹										
닢	닢	닢	닢										
딭	딭	딭	딭										
릭	릭	릭	릭										
및	및	및	및										
빗	빗	빗	빗										
싱	싱	싱	싱										
잇	잇	잇	잇										
집	집	집	집										
침	침	침	침										
킬	킬	킬	킬										
틷	틷	틷	틷										
핀	핀	핀	핀										
힉	힉	힉	힉										

Consonants +ㅡ

Consonants +ー+ ending consonant

흥 | 흥 | 흥 | 흥
늎 | 늎 | 늎 | 늎
듵 | 듵 | 듵 | 듵
릌 | 릌 | 릌 | 릌
믗 | 믗 | 믗 | 믗
븇 | 븇 | 븇 | 븇
승 | 승 | 승 | 승
읏 | 읏 | 읏 | 읏
즙 | 즙 | 즙 | 즙
츰 | 츰 | 츰 | 츰
클 | 클 | 클 | 클
튼 | 튼 | 튼 | 튼
픈 | 픈 | 픈 | 픈
흑 | 흑 | 흑 | 흑

Consonants + ㅐ

개 | 개 개 개 | | | | | | | | | |
내 | 내 내 내 | | | | | | | | | |
대 | 대 대 대 | | | | | | | | | |
래 | 래 래 래 | | | | | | | | | |
매 | 매 매 매 | | | | | | | | | |
배 | 배 배 배 | | | | | | | | | |
새 | 새 새 새 | | | | | | | | | |
애 | 애 애 애 | | | | | | | | | |
재 | 재 재 재 | | | | | | | | | |
채 | 채 채 채 | | | | | | | | | |
캐 | 캐 캐 캐 | | | | | | | | | |
태 | 태 태 태 | | | | | | | | | |
패 | 패 패 패 | | | | | | | | | |
해 | 해 해 해 | | | | | | | | | |

Consonants + ㅐ + ending consonant

갱 | 갱 | 갱 | 갱 | | | | | | | | |

냅 | 냅 | 냅 | 냅 | | | | | | | | |

댙 | 댙 | 댙 | 댙 | | | | | | | | |

랙 | 랙 | 랙 | 랙 | | | | | | | | |

맺 | 맺 | 맺 | 맺 | | | | | | | | |

뱃 | 뱃 | 뱃 | 뱃 | | | | | | | | |

생 | 생 | 생 | 생 | | | | | | | | |

앳 | 앳 | 앳 | 앳 | | | | | | | | |

잽 | 잽 | 잽 | 잽 | | | | | | | | |

챔 | 챔 | 챔 | 챔 | | | | | | | | |

캘 | 캘 | 캘 | 캘 | | | | | | | | |

탠 | 탠 | 탠 | 탠 | | | | | | | | |

팬 | 팬 | 팬 | 팬 | | | | | | | | |

핵 | 핵 | 핵 | 핵 | | | | | | | | |

Consonants + ㅔ

게	게	게	게								
네	네	네	네								
데	데	데	데								
레	레	레	레								
메	메	메	메								
베	베	베	베								
세	세	세	세								
에	에	에	에								
제	제	제	제								
체	체	체	체								
케	케	케	케								
테	테	테	테								
페	페	페	페								
헤	헤	헤	헤								

Consonants + ㅔ + ending consonant

겡	겡	겡	겡								
넒	넒	넒	넒								
뎉	뎉	뎉	뎉								
렉	렉	렉	렉								
멫	멫	멫	멫								
벳	벳	벳	벳								
셍	셍	셍	셍								
엣	엣	엣	엣								
젭	젭	젭	젭								
쳄	쳄	쳄	쳄								
켈	켈	켈	켈								
텥	텥	텥	텥								
펜	펜	펜	펜								
헥	헥	헥	헥								

개	걔	걔	걔								
내	냬	냬	냬								
대	댸	댸	댸								
래	럐	럐	럐								
매	먜	먜	먜								
배	뱨	뱨	뱨								
섀	섀	섀	섀								
얘	얘	얘	얘								
쟤	쟤	쟤	쟤								
챼	챼	챼	챼								
컈	컈	컈	컈								
턔	턔	턔	턔								
퍠	퍠	퍠	퍠								
햬	햬	햬	햬								

Consonants + ㅐ + ending consonant

갱	갱	갱	갱								
냴	냴	냴	냴								
댙	댙	댙	댙								
랙	랙	랙	랙								
맺	맺	맺	맺								
뱆	뱆	뱆	뱆								
생	생	생	생								
앳	앳	앳	앳								
잽	잽	잽	잽								
챔	챔	챔	챔								
캘	캘	캘	캘								
탙	탙	탙	탙								
팬	팬	팬	팬								
핵	핵	핵	핵								

계 계 계 계

녜 녜 녜 녜

뎨 뎨 뎨 뎨

례 례 례 례

몌 몌 몌 몌

볘 볘 볘 볘

셰 셰 셰 셰

예 예 예 예

졔 졔 졔 졔

쳬 쳬 쳬 쳬

켸 켸 켸 켸

톄 톄 톄 톄

폐 폐 폐 폐

혜 혜 혜 혜

Consonants + ㅖ + ending consonant

곕	곕	곕	곕									
녤	녤	녤	녤									
뎉	뎉	뎉	뎉									
롁	롁	롁	롁									
몟	몟	몟	몟									
뼷	뼷	뼷	뼷									
솅	솅	솅	솅									
옛	옛	옛	옛									
곕	졉	졉	졉									
쳼	쳼	쳼	쳼									
켈	켈	켈	켈									
톝	톝	톝	톝									
폩	폩	폩	폩									
혝	혝	혝	혝									

Consonants +ㅘ

과 | 과 과 과
뇌 | 놔 놔 놔
돠 | 돠 돠 돠
롸 | 롸 롸 롸
뫄 | 뫄 뫄 뫄
봐 | 봐 봐 봐
솨 | 솨 솨 솨
와 | 와 와 와
좌 | 좌 좌 좌
촤 | 촤 촤 촤
콰 | 콰 콰 콰
톼 | 톼 톼 톼
퐈 | 퐈 퐈 퐈
화 | 화 화 화

Consonants +ㅘ+ ending consonant

괗	괗	괗	괗								
놢	놢	놢	놢								
돹	돹	돹	돹								
뢐	뢐	뢐	뢐								
뫚	뫚	뫚	뫚								
봧	봧	봧	봧								
쌍	쌍	쌍	쌍								
왓	왓	왓	왓								
좝	좝	좝	좝								
촴	촴	촴	촴								
콸	콸	콸	콸								
퇄	퇄	퇄	퇄								
퐌	퐌	퐌	퐌								
확	확	확	확								

괘	괘	괘	괘									
놰	놰	놰	놰									
돼	돼	돼	돼									
뢔	뢔	뢔	뢔									
뫠	뫠	뫠	뫠									
봬	봬	봬	봬									
쇄	쇄	쇄	쇄									
왜	왜	왜	왜									
좨	좨	좨	좨									
쵀	쵀	쵀	쵀									
쾌	쾌	쾌	쾌									
퇘	퇘	퇘	퇘									
퐤	퐤	퐤	퐤									
홰	홰	홰	홰									

Consonants +ㅙ+ ending consonant

괙 | 괙 괙 괙
넓 | 넓 넓 넓
뙡 | 뙡 뙡 뙡
뢬 | 뢬 뢬 뢬
뫛 | 뫛 뫛 뫛
뿻 | 뿻 뿻 뿻
쇙 | 쇙 쇙 쇙
왯 | 왯 왯 왯
좹 | 좹 좹 좹
쵐 | 쵐 쵐 쵐
쾔 | 쾔 쾔 쾔
퇕 | 퇕 퇕 퇕
퐨 | 퐨 퐨 퐨
홱 | 홱 홱 홱

괴	괴	괴	괴								
뇌	뇌	뇌	뇌								
되	되	되	되								
뢰	뢰	뢰	뢰								
뫼	뫼	뫼	뫼								
뵈	뵈	뵈	뵈								
쇠	쇠	쇠	쇠								
외	외	외	외								
죄	죄	죄	죄								
최	최	최	최								
쾨	쾨	쾨	쾨								
퇴	퇴	퇴	퇴								
푀	푀	푀	푀								
회	회	회	회								

Consonants + ㅚ + ending consonant

굉	굉	굉	굉								
뇨	뇨	뇨	뇨								
된	된	된	된								
뢱	뢱	뢱	뢱								
묏	묏	묏	묏								
뷧	뷧	뷧	뷧								
쇵	쇵	쇵	쇵								
욋	욋	욋	욋								
줩	줩	줩	줩								
쵬	쵬	쵬	쵬								
쾰	쾰	쾰	쾰								
퇻	퇻	퇻	퇻								
푄	푄	푄	푄								
획	획	획	획								

궈	궈	궈	궈									
눠	눠	눠	눠									
둬	둬	둬	둬									
뤄	뤄	뤄	뤄									
뭐	뭐	뭐	뭐									
붜	붜	붜	붜									
쉬	쉬	쉬	쉬									
워	워	워	워									
줘	줘	줘	줘									
춰	춰	춰	춰									
쿼	쿼	쿼	쿼									
퉈	퉈	퉈	퉈									
풔	풔	풔	풔									
훠	훠	훠	훠									

Consonants +ㅝ+ ending consonant

궝 | 궝 | 궝 | 궝
뉞 | 뉞 | 뉞 | 뉞
뒽 | 뒽 | 뒽 | 뒽
뤜 | 뤜 | 뤜 | 뤜
뭧 | 뭧 | 뭧 | 뭧
붲 | 붲 | 붲 | 붲
쉉 | 쉉 | 쉉 | 쉉
윗 | 윗 | 윗 | 윗
줩 | 줩 | 줩 | 줩
췸 | 췸 | 췸 | 췸
퀄 | 퀄 | 퀄 | 퀄
퉡 | 퉡 | 퉡 | 퉡
풘 | 풘 | 풘 | 풘
훡 | 훡 | 훡 | 훡

Consonants +ㅞ

궤 | 궤 | 궤 | 궤 | | | | | | | | | |
눼 | 눼 | 눼 | 눼 | | | | | | | | | |
뒈 | 뒈 | 뒈 | 뒈 | | | | | | | | | |
뤠 | 뤠 | 뤠 | 뤠 | | | | | | | | | |
뭬 | 뭬 | 뭬 | 뭬 | | | | | | | | | |
붸 | 붸 | 붸 | 붸 | | | | | | | | | |
쉐 | 쉐 | 쉐 | 쉐 | | | | | | | | | |
웨 | 웨 | 웨 | 웨 | | | | | | | | | |
줴 | 줴 | 줴 | 줴 | | | | | | | | | |
췌 | 췌 | 췌 | 췌 | | | | | | | | | |
퀘 | 퀘 | 퀘 | 퀘 | | | | | | | | | |
퉤 | 퉤 | 퉤 | 퉤 | | | | | | | | | |
풰 | 풰 | 풰 | 풰 | | | | | | | | | |
훼 | 훼 | 훼 | 훼 | | | | | | | | | |

Consonants +ㅞ+ ending consonant

궹 궹 궹 궹

뉖 뉖 뉖 뉖

뒡 뒡 뒡 뒡

뤡 뤡 뤡 뤡

뭿 뭿 뭿 뭿

뷋 뷋 뷋 뷋

쉥 쉥 쉥 쉥

웻 웻 웻 웻

쥅 쥅 쥅 쥅

췜 췜 췜 췜

퀠 퀠 퀠 퀠

퉨 퉨 퉨 퉨

풴 풴 풴 풴

훽 훽 훽 훽

Consonants +ㅟ

귀 | 귀 | 귀 | 귀 | | | | | | | |
뉘 | 뉘 | 뉘 | 뉘 | | | | | | | |
뒤 | 뒤 | 뒤 | 뒤 | | | | | | | |
뤼 | 뤼 | 뤼 | 뤼 | | | | | | | |
뮈 | 뮈 | 뮈 | 뮈 | | | | | | | |
뷔 | 뷔 | 뷔 | 뷔 | | | | | | | |
쉬 | 쉬 | 쉬 | 쉬 | | | | | | | |
위 | 위 | 위 | 위 | | | | | | | |
쥐 | 쥐 | 쥐 | 쥐 | | | | | | | |
취 | 취 | 취 | 취 | | | | | | | |
퀴 | 퀴 | 퀴 | 퀴 | | | | | | | |
튀 | 튀 | 튀 | 튀 | | | | | | | |
퓌 | 퓌 | 퓌 | 퓌 | | | | | | | |
휘 | 휘 | 휘 | 휘 | | | | | | | |

Consonants +ㅟ+ ending consonant

쿵	쿵	쿵	쿵								
늪	늪	늪	늪								
뒽	뒽	뒽	뒽								
뤅	뤅	뤅	뤅								
뮞	뮞	뮞	뮞								
뷪	뷪	뷪	뷪								
싱	싱	싱	싱								
윗	윗	윗	윗								
줩	줩	줩	줩								
춰	춰	춰	춰								
퀄	퀄	퀄	퀄								
튈	튈	튈	튈								
퓐	퓐	퓐	퓐								
휔	휔	휔	휔								

긔 긔 긔 긔

늬 늬 늬 늬

듸 듸 듸 듸

릐 릐 릐 릐

믜 믜 믜 믜

븨 븨 븨 븨

싀 싀 싀 싀

의 의 의 의

즤 즤 즤 즤

츼 츼 츼 츼

킈 킈 킈 킈

틔 틔 틔 틔

픠 픠 픠 픠

희 희 희 희

Consonants + ─| + ending consonant

킁	킁	킁	킁								
닢	닢	닢	닢								
딭	딭	딭	딭								
릭	릭	릭	릭								
및	및	및	및								
빛	빛	빛	빛								
싱	싱	싱	싱								
잇	잇	잇	잇								
집	집	집	집								
침	침	침	침								
킬	킬	킬	킬								
틭	틭	틭	틭								
핀	핀	핀	핀								
획	획	획	획								

Double consonants + ㅏ

까 | 까 까 까
따 | 따 따 따
빠 | 빠 빠 빠
짜 | 짜 짜 짜
싸 | 싸 싸 싸

Double consonants + ㅏ + ending consonant

깍 | 깍 깍 깍
딴 | 딴 딴 딴
빤 | 빤 빤 빤
짤 | 짤 짤 짤
쌈 | 쌈 쌈 쌈
깝 | 깝 깝 깝
땃 | 땃 땃 땃
빵 | 빵 빵 빵

Double consonants + ㅏ

까 | 까 까 까
따 | 따 따 따
빠 | 빠 빠 빠
짜 | 짜 짜 짜
싸 | 싸 싸 싸

Double consonants + ㅏ + ending consonant

깟 | 깟 깟 깟
땅 | 땅 땅 땅
빴 | 빴 빴 빴
짲 | 짲 짲 짲
싹 | 싹 싹 싹
깥 | 깥 깥 깥
땊 | 땊 땊 땊
빵 | 빵 빵 빵

Double consonants + ㅓ

꺼 꺼 꺼 꺼

떠 떠 떠 떠

뻐 뻐 뻐 뻐

쩌 쩌 쩌 쩌

써 써 써 써

Double consonants + ㅓ + ending consonant

꺽 꺽 꺽 꺽

떤 떤 떤 떤

뻔 뻔 뻔 뻔

쩔 쩔 쩔 쩔

썸 썸 썸 썸

껍 껍 껍 껍

떳 떳 떳 떳

뻥 뻥 뻥 뻥

Double consonants + ㅕ

껴 껴 껴 껴

떠 떠 떠 떠

뼈 뼈 뼈 뼈

쪄 쪄 쪄 쪄

쎠 쎠 쎠 쎠

Double consonants + ㅕ + ending consonant

껷 껷 껷 껷

떻 떻 떻 떻

뼷 뼷 뼷 뼷

쪾 쪾 쪾 쪾

쎰 쎰 쎰 쎰

껼 껼 껼 껼

떺 떺 떺 떺

뼝 뼝 뼝 뼝

Double consonants +ㅗ

꼬

또

뽀

쪼

쏘

Double consonants +ㅗ+ ending consonant

꼭

똔

뽈

쫄

쏨

꼽

똣

뽕

93

Double consonants +ㅛ

꾜	꾜	꾜	꾜									
뚀	뚀	뚀	뚀									
뾰	뾰	뾰	뾰									
쬬	쬬	쬬	쬬									
쏘	쏘	쏘	쏘									

Double consonants +ㅛ+ ending consonant

꾝	꾝	꾝	꾝					
뚕	뚕	뚕	뚕					
뾱	뾱	뾱	뾱					
쬧	쬧	쬧	쬧					
쑉	쑉	쑉	쑉					
꾙	꾙	꾙	꾙					
뚚	뚚	뚚	뚚					
뾷	뾷	뾷	뾷					

Double consonants +ㅜ

꾸

뚜

뿌

쭈

쑤

Double consonants +ㅜ+ ending consonant

꾹

뚠

뿐

쭐

쑴

꿉

뜻

뿡

Double consonants +ㅠ

꾸 　꾸 꾸 꾸

뜌 　뜌 뜌 뜌

뿨 　뿨 뿨 뿨

쮸 　쮸 쮸 쮸

쓔 　쓔 쓔 쓔

Double consonants +ㅠ+ ending consonant

꾰 　꾰 꾰 꾰

뜕 　뜕 뜕 뜕

뿊 　뿊 뿊 뿊

쮲 　쮲 쮲 쮲

쓖 　쓖 쓖 쓖

꾶 　꾶 꾶 꾶

뜚 　뜚 뜚 뜚

뿛 　뿛 뿛 뿛

Double consonants + ㅣ

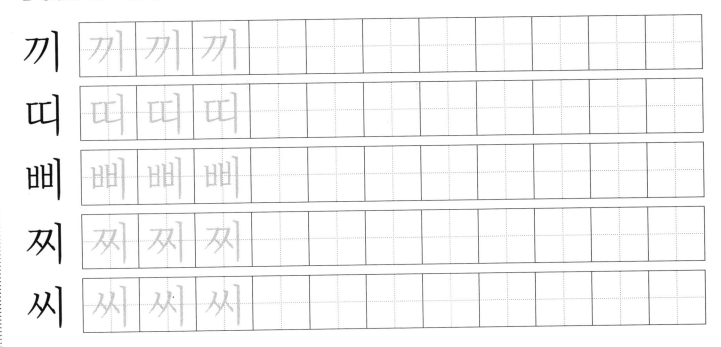

끼 | 끼 | 끼 | 끼
띠 | 띠 | 띠 | 띠
삐 | 삐 | 삐 | 삐
찌 | 찌 | 찌 | 찌
씨 | 씨 | 씨 | 씨

Double consonants + ㅣ + ending consonant

끽 | 끽 | 끽 | 끽
띤 | 띤 | 띤 | 띤
삔 | 삔 | 삔 | 삔
찔 | 찔 | 찔 | 찔
씸 | 씸 | 씸 | 씸
낍 | 낍 | 낍 | 낍
띳 | 띳 | 띳 | 띳
삥 | 삥 | 삥 | 삥

Double consonants +ㅡ

꼬 | ㄲ ㄲ ㄲ

뜨 | ㄸ ㄸ ㄸ

쁘 | ㅃ ㅃ ㅃ

쯔 | ㅉ ㅉ ㅉ

쓰 | ㅆ ㅆ ㅆ

Double consonants +ㅡ+ ending consonant

끗 | 끗 끗 끗

뜽 | 뜽 뜽 뜽

쁫 | 쁫 쁫 쁫

쫓 | 쫓 쫓 쫓

쓱 | 쓱 쓱 쓱

끝 | 끝 끝 끝

뜦 | 뜦 뜦 뜦

쁠 | 쁠 쁠 쁠

Double consonants + ㅐ

깨 깨 깨 깨

때 때 때 때

빼 빼 빼 빼

째 째 째 째

쌔 쌔 쌔 쌔

Double consonants + ㅐ + ending consonant

깩 깩 깩 깩

땐 땐 땐 땐

뻰 뻰 뻰 뻰

짤 짤 짤 짤

쌤 쌤 쌤 쌤

깹 깹 깹 깹

땟 땟 땟 땟

빵 빵 빵 빵

Double consonants + ㅔ

께	께	께	께
떼	떼	떼	떼
뻬	뻬	뻬	뻬
쩨	쩨	쩨	쩨
쎄	쎄	쎄	쎄

Double consonants + ㅔ + ending consonant

껫	껫	껫	껫
뗑	뗑	뗑	뗑
뻿	뻿	뻿	뻿
쩻	쩻	쩻	쩻
쎅	쎅	쎅	쎅
껱	껱	껱	껱
뗇	뗇	뗇	뗇
뼁	뼁	뼁	뼁

Double consonants + ㅐ

깨 | 깨 깨 깨

때 | 때 때 때

빼 | 빼 빼 빼

째 | 째 째 째

쌔 | 쌔 쌔 쌔

Double consonants + ㅐ + ending consonant

깩 | 깩 깩 깩

땐 | 땐 땐 땐

뺀 | 뺀 뺀 뺀

쨀 | 쨀 쨀 쨀

쌤 | 쌤 쌤 쌤

깹 | 깹 깹 깹

땟 | 땟 땟 땟

뺑 | 뺑 뺑 뺑

Double consonants + ㅖ

꼐 꼐 꼐 꼐

뗴 뗴 뗴 뗴

뻬 뻬 뻬 뻬

쪠 쪠 쪠 쪠

쎼 쎼 쎼 쎼

Double consonants + ㅖ + ending consonant

꼣 꼣 꼣 꼣

뗑 뗑 뗑 뗑

뻿 뻿 뻿 뻿

쪳 쪳 쪳 쪳

쎽 쎽 쎽 쎽

꼩 꼩 꼩 꼩

뗥 뗥 뗥 뗥

뻥 뻥 뻥 뻥

Double consonants +ㅘ

꽈 꽈 꽈 꽈

똬 똬 똬 똬

뽜 뽜 뽜 뽜

쫘 쫘 쫘 쫘

쏴 쏴 쏴 쏴

Double consonants +ㅘ+ ending consonant

꽉 꽉 꽉 꽉

똰 똰 똰 똰

뽠 뽠 뽠 뽠

쫠 쫠 쫠 쫠

쐄 쐄 쐄 쐄

꽙 꽙 꽙 꽙

똿 똿 똿 똿

뽱 뽱 뽱 뽱

Double consonants +ㅙ

꽤 | 꽤 꽤 꽤

때 | 때 때 때

빼 | 빼 빼 빼

쫴 | 쫴 쫴 쫴

쐐 | 쐐 쐐 쐐

Double consonants +ㅙ+ ending consonant

꽷 | 꽷 꽷 꽷

땡 | 땡 땡 땡

뺏 | 뺏 뺏 뺏

쫮 | 쫮 쫮 쫮

쐭 | 쐭 쐭 쐭

꽽 | 꽽 꽽 꽽

땳 | 땳 땳 땳

뺑 | 뺑 뺑 뺑

Double consonants +ㅚ

꾀
뙤
뾔
쬐
쐬

Double consonants +ㅚ+ ending consonant

꾁
뙨
뾘
쬘
쐼
꾑
뙷
뾩

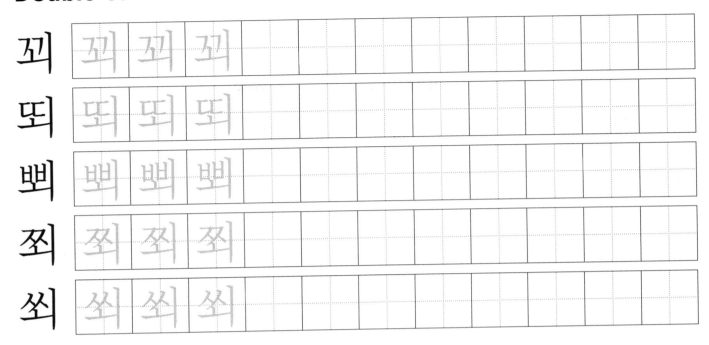

Double consonants +ㅝ

꿔 꿔 꿔 꿔

뚸 뚸 뚸 뚸

뿨 뿨 뿨 뿨

쭤 쭤 쭤 쭤

쒀 쒀 쒀 쒀

Double consonants +ㅝ+ ending consonant

꿧 꿧 꿧 꿧

뚱 뚱 뚱 뚱

뿣 뿣 뿣 뿣

쭢 쭢 쭢 쭢

쒁 쒁 쒁 쒁

꿭 꿭 꿭 꿭

뚫 뚫 뚫 뚫

뿽 뿽 뿽 뿽

Double consonants +ㅞ

꿰

뛔

뿨

쮀

쒜

Double consonants +ㅞ+ ending consonant

꿱

뛘

뿰

쮈

쒬

꿥

뛧

뿽

Double consonants +ㅟ

꿰 꿰 꿰 꿰

뛰 뛰 뛰 뛰

쀠 쀠 쀠 쀠

쮀 쮀 쮀 쮀

쒸 쒸 쒸 쒸

Double consonants +ㅟ+ ending consonant

꿧 꿧 꿧 꿧

뛩 뛩 뛩 뛩

쀳 쀳 쀳 쀳

쮖 쮖 쮖 쮖

쒹 쒹 쒹 쒹

꿽 꿽 꿽 꿽

뛺 뛺 뛺 뛺

쀵 쀵 쀵 쀵

Double consonants + ㅢ

끼
띠
삐
찌
씨

Double consonants + ㅢ + ending consonant

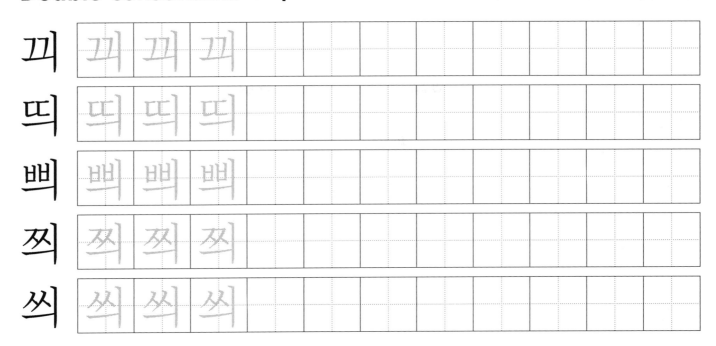

끽
띤
삗
찔
씸
낍
띳
뺑

Four-letter syllables

갉 갉 갉 갉

냤 냤 냤 냤

덟 덟 덟 덟

렶 렶 렶 렶

몴 몴 몴 몴

뵶 뵶 뵶 뵶

숡 숡 숡 숡

윲 윲 윲 윲

짉 짉 짉 짉

츴 츴 츴 츴

캢 캢 캢 캢

텘 텘 텘 텘

퍲 퍲 퍲 퍲

혥 혥 혥 혥

단어 쓰기 연습

Words Writing Practice

Useful phrases / 유용한 구절

Yes [ne]

네

No [anio]

아니오

Goog morning! [annyeonghaseyo]

안녕하세요

Thank you [gomabseubnida]

고맙습니다

You're welcome [cheonman-eyo]

천만에요

Excuse me! (apology) [sillyehabnida]

실례합니다

It's okay! [gwaenchanh-ayo]

괜찮아요

I don't know [mollayo]

몰라요

Sorry [mianhabnida]

미안합니다

Goodbye (to person leaving) [annyeonghi gaseyo]

안녕히가세요

Goodbye (to person staying) [annyeonghi gyeseyo]

안녕히계세요

Maybe [amado]

아마도

Just a moment! [jamkkanman-yo!]

잠깐만요!

How much is this? [igeo eolmayeyo?]

이거얼마예요?

Please repeat that [dasi malhae juseyo]

다시말해주세요

Please speak slowly [cheoncheonhi malhae juseyo]

천천히말해주세요

Please write it down [jeog-eo juseyo]

적어주세요

I understand [ihaehaeyo]

이해해요

I don't understand [ihae moshaeyo]

이해못해요

I don't know [mollayo]

몰라요

I know [al-ayo]

알아요

Good [joh-ayo]

좋아요

Bad [an joh-ayo]

안좋아요

Colors / 그림 물감

Gold [geumsaeg]

금색

Silver [eunsaeg]

은색

Black [geom-eunsaeg]

검은색

White [hayansaeg]

하얀색

Gray [hoesaeg]

회색

Green [chologsaeg]

초록색

Blue [palansaeg]

파란색

Yellow [nolansaeg]

노란색

Pink [bunhongsaeg]

분홍색

Orange [juhwangsaeg]

주황색

Brown [galsaeg]

갈색

Maroon [jeoggalsaeg]

적 갈 색

Sky Blue [haneulsaeg]

하 늘 색

Red [ppalgansaeg]

빨 간 색

Beige [beijisaeg]

베 이 지 색

Ivory [aibolisaeg]

아 이 보 리 색

Apricot [salgusaeg]

살 구 색

Purple [bolasaeg]

보 라 색

Light Yellow [yeonnolansaeg]

연 노 란 색

Green (Khaki) [kakisaeg]

카 키 색

Turquoise [cheonglogsaeg]

청 록 색

Light Green [yeondusaeg]

연 두 색

Indigo [namsaeg]

남 색

Family / 가족

Parents [bumonim]

부모님

Father [abeoji]

아버지

Dad [appa]

아빠

Mother [eomeoni]

어머니

Mom [eomma]

엄마

Couple [bubu]

부부

Spouse [baeuja]

배우자

Husband (formal) [nampyeon]

남편

Groom [sinlang]

신랑

Wife (formal) [anae]

아내

Bride [sinbu]

신부

Siblings, brothers and sisters [hyeongjejamae]

형제자매

Older brother (used by males) [hyeong]

형

Older brother (used by females) [oppa]

오빠

Older sister (used by males) [nuna]

누나

Older sister (used by females) [eonni]

언니

Younger sibling [dongsaeng]

동생

Younger brother [namdongsaeng]

남동생

Younger sister [yeodongsaeng]

여동생

Son [adeul]

아들

Daughter [ttal]

딸

Baby [agi]

아기

Grandparents [jobumo]

조부모

Grandfather (father's father) [hal-abeoji]

할아버지

Grandmother (father's mother) [halmeoni]

할머니

Grandfather (mother's father) [oehal-abeoji]

외할아버지

Grandmother (mother's mother) [oehalmeoni]

외할머니

Uncle [samchon]

삼촌

Aunt (father's sister) [gomo]

고모

Aunt (mother's sister) [imo]

이모

Nephew [joka]

조카

Niece [jokattal]

조카딸

Grandson [sonja]

손자

Granddaughter [sonnyeo]

손녀

Cousin [sachon]

사촌

House / 집

House [jib]

집

Room [bang]

방

Bathroom [hwajangsil]

화장실

Kitchen [bueok]

부엌

Living room [geosil]

거실

Bedroom [chimsil]

침실

Balcony [balkoni]

발코니

Backyard [dwismadang]

뒷마당

Stairs [gyedan]

계단

Attic [dalagbang]

다락방

Apartment [apateu]

아파트

Professions / 직업

Plumber [baegwangong]

배관공

Carpenter [mogsu]

목수

Gardener [jeong-wonsa]

정원사

Locksmith [yeolsoegong]

열쇠공

Real estate agent [budongsan-eobja]

부동산업자

Electrician [jeongi os]

전기 기술자

Painter (of walls) [peinteu gong]

페인트공

Sculptor [jogagga]

조각가

Company worker [hoesawon]

회사원

Housewife [jubu]

주부

Pilot [pailleos]

파일럿

Flight attendant [seungmuwon]

승무원

Painter (artist) [hwaga]

화가

Computer programmer [peulogeulaemeo]

프로그래머

Farmer [nongbu]

농부

Doctor [uisa]

의사

Dentist [chigwa uisa]

치과의사

Veterinarian [suuisa]

수의사

Nurse [ganhosa]

간호사

Translator [beon-yeogga]

번역가

Lawyer [byeonhosa]

변호사

Soldier [gun-in]

군인

Driver [unjeonbyeong]

운전병

Teacher, mentor [seuseung]

스승

Student [hagsaeng]

학생

Professor [gyosu]

교수

Singer [gasu]

가수

Composer [jaggogga]

작곡가

Photographer [sajinsa]

사진사

Police officer [gyeongchalgwan]

경찰관

Poet [siin]

시인

Writer [jagga]

작가

Reporter [gija]

기자

Architect [geonchugga]

건축가

Builder [geonchug-eobja]

건축업자

Food and drinks / 음식과 음료

Kimchi [gimchi]

김치

Cooked White Rice [bab]

밥

Rice with beans [kongbab]

콩밥

Kimchi Fried Rice [gimchi bokk-eumbab]

김치볶음밥

Stir-fried [bokk-eum]

볶음

Stir-Fried Pork [jeyug bokk-eum]

제육볶음

Porridge [jug]

죽

Stew [jjigae]

찌개

Soup [gug]

국

Hot Pot [jeongol]

전골

Meat [gogi]

고기

Noodles [gugsu]

국 수

Noodle Soup [kalgugsu]

칼 국 수

Pancake [jeon]

전

Side dishes [banchan]

반 찬

Alcohol [sul]

술

Beer [maegju]

맥 주

Water [mul]

물

Green Tea [nogcha]

녹 차

Black tea [hongcha]

홍 차

Breakfast [achim sigsa]

아 침 식 사

Lunch [jeomsim]

점 심

Dinner [jeonyeog sigsa]

저 녁 식 사

Animals / 동물

Dog [gae]

개

Puppy [gang-aji]

강아지

Cat [goyang-i]

고양이

Cow [so]

소

Horse [mal]

말

Zebra [eollugmal]

얼룩말

Donkey [dangnagwi]

당나귀

Tiger [holang-i]

호랑이

Lion [saja]

사자

Cheetah [chita]

치타

Wolf [neugdae]

늑대

Pig [dwaeji]

돼지

Wild boar [mesdwaeji]

멧돼지

Sheep [yang]

양

Goat [yeomso]

염소

Kangaroo [kaeng-geolu]

캥거루

Deer [saseum]

사슴

Rabbit [tokki]

토끼

Giraffe [gilin]

기린

monkey [wonsung-i]

원숭이

Elephant [kokkili]

코끼리

Bear [gom]

곰

Squirrel [dalamjwi]

다람쥐

Date and time / 날짜와 시간

Second [cho]
초

Minute [bun]
분

Hour [si]
시

Time [sigan]
시간

Day [il]
일

Week [ju]
주

Month [wol]
월

Year [nyeon]
년

Today [oneul]
오늘

Tomorrow [naeil]
내일

Yesterday [eoje]
어제

Sunday [il-yoil]

일요일

Monday [wol-yoil]

월요일

Tuesday [hwayoil]

화요일

Wednesday [suyoil]

수요일

Thursday [mog-yoil]

목요일

Friday [geum-yoil]

금요일

Saturday [toyoil]

토요일

Morning (AM) [ojeon]

오전

Afternoon (PM) [ohu]

오후

Last week [ibeonju]

이번주

Next week [da-eumju]

다음주

Every week [maeju]

매주

City / 시티

Theater [yeonghwagwan]

영화관

Cafe [keopi syob]

커피숍

Bookstore [seojeom]

서점

Hospital [byeong-won]

병원

Clothing store [osgage]

옷 가게

Restaurant [sigdang]

식당

Bank [eunhaeng]

은행

Airport [gonghang]

공항

Toilets [hwajangsil]

화장실

Car park [juchajang]

주차장

Stationery shop [munbang-gu]

문방구

Shop [gage]

가게

Fruit store [gwail gage]

과일가게

Vegetable store [yachae gage]

야채가게

Public market [sijang]

시장

Zoo [dongmul-won]

동물원

Supermarket [daehyeong mateu]

대형마트

Convenience store [pyeon-uijeom]

편의점

Public sauna [jjimjilbang]

찜질방

Playground [undongjang]

운동장

Fitness club [helseu keulleob]

헬스클럽

Park [gong-won]

공원

Beauty salon [miyongsil]

미용실

Clothes and fashion / 옷과 패션

Traditional Korean clothing [hanbog]

한 복

Business suit [yangbog]

양 복

Suit [jeongjang]

정 장

Hat [moja]

모 자

Glasses [angyeong]

안 경

Sunglasses [seongeullaseu]

선 글 라 스

Shirt [tisyeocheu]

티 셔 츠

Dress shirt [wai syeocheu]

와 이 셔 츠

Coat [koteu]

코 트

Jumper [jeompeo]

점 퍼

Jacket [jakes]

자 켓

Upper garments [wis-os]

윗 옷

Belt [belteu]

벨 트

Pants [baji]

바 지

Shorts [geot-os]

반 바 지

Jeans [cheongbaji]

청 바 지

Skirt [chima]

치 마

Sports shoes [undonghwa]

운 동 화

High-heeled shoes [haihil]

하 이 힐

Shoes [sinbal]

신 발

Dress shoes [gudu]

구 두

Socks [yangmal]

양 말

Boots [boda]

부 츠

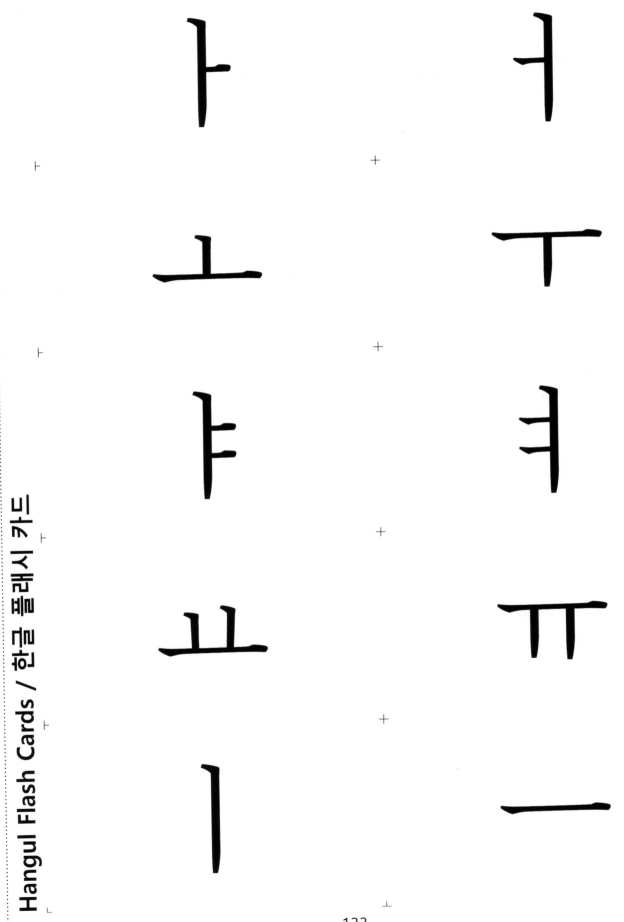

어 [eo]

Pronunciation: [eo]

아 [a]

Pronunciation: [a]

우 [u]

Pronunciation: [u]

오 [o]

Pronunciation: [o]

여 [yeo]

Pronunciation: [yeo]

야 [ya]

Pronunciation: [ya]

유 [yu]

Pronunciation: [yu]

요 [yo]

Pronunciation: [yo]

으 [eu]

Pronunciation: [eu]

이 [i]

Pronunciation: [i]

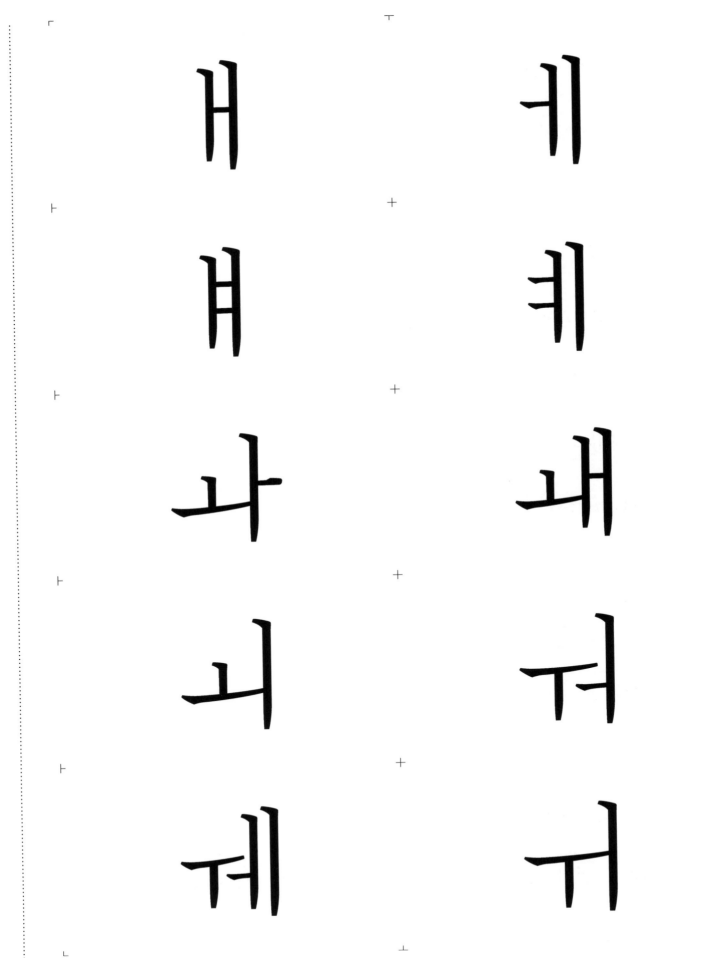

에 [e]

Pronunciation: [e]

애 [ae]

Pronunciation: [ae]

예 [ye]

Pronunciation: [ye]

얘 [yae]

Pronunciation: [yae]

왜 [wae]

Pronunciation: [wae]

와 [wa]

Pronunciation: [wa]

워 [wo]

Pronunciation: [wo]

외 [oe]

Pronunciation: [oe]

위 [wi]

Pronunciation: [wi]

웨 [we]

Pronunciation: [we]

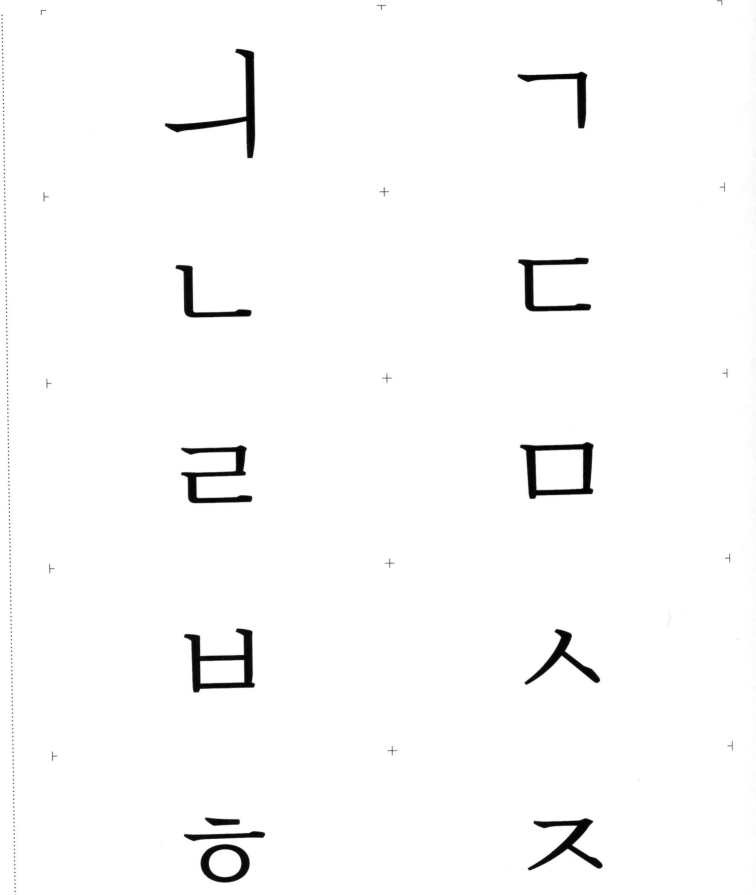

기역 [gi-yeok]

Pronunciation: [g/-k]

의 [ui]

Pronunciation: [ui]

디귿 [di-geut]

Pronunciation: [d/-t]

니은 [ni-eun]

Pronunciation: [n]

미음 [mi-eum]

Pronunciation: [m]

리을 [ri-eul/li-eul]

Pronunciation: [r/-l]

시옷 [shi-ot]

Pronunciation: [s]

비읍 [bi-eup]

Pronunciation: [b/-p]

지읏 [ji-eut]

Pronunciation: [j]

히읗 [hi-eu/hi-eut]

Pronunciation: [h]

ㅋ

ㅍ

ㅇ

ㄸ

ㅉ

ㅌ

ㅊ

ㄲ

ㅃ

ㅆ

티읕 [ti-eut]

Pronunciation: [t]

키읔 [ki-euk]

Pronunciation: [k]

치읓 [chi-eut]

Pronunciation: [ch]

피읖 [pi-eup]

Pronunciation: [p]

쌍기역 [ssang-giyeok]

Pronunciation: [gg/-kk]

이응 [i-eung]

Pronunciation: [- / -ng]

쌍비읍 [ssang-bi-eup]

Pronunciation: [bb/-pp]

쌍디귿 [ssang-digeut]

Pronunciation: [dd/-tt]

쌍시옷 [ssang-si-ot]

Pronunciation: [ss]

쌍지읒 [ssang-ji-eut]

Pronunciation: [jj]

Finished learning Hangul but want to know more about Korean writing? Learn to write Hanja characters!

Hanja is the Korean name for a traditional writing system consisting mainly of Traditional Chinese characters incorporated into the Korean language with Korean pronunciation. These days it is not necessary to learn Hanja to be able to understand Korean; however as the system of Chinese characters has been in use for centuries in Korea a lot of words are rooted in Hanja. Thus knowing these characters will allow you to better understand the language and the etymology of words. Also - let's face it - Hanja is simply cool!

At the moment with have 2 Hanja Writing Workbooks available for sale:

Together they contain over 180 Hanja characters for you to learn and practice writing. Here's just one of them:

meaning	**Korea**
readnings	나라 이름 한
romanization	[nala ileum han]
compounds	北韓 북한 [bughan] North Korea
	韓國 한국 [hangug] Korea
	韓國語 한국어 [hangug-eo] Korean (language)

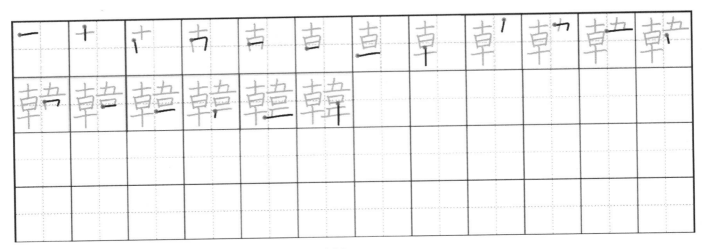

Our Hanja workbooks also contain some of the Korean words that can be written using Traditional Chinese Characters. Here's an example of a practice page:

대학교 [daehaggyo] college, university

大學校

인생 [insaeng] life

人生

남대문 [namdaemun] Seoul's old south gate

南大門

입국 [ibgug] entering a country

入國

일월 [il-wol] January

一月

학교 [haggyo] school

學校

일대 [ildae] great, remarkable

一大

유월 [yuwol] June

六月

북한 [bughan] North Korea

北韓

국민 [gugmin] citizen

國民

시월 [siwol] October

十月

Made in the USA
Columbia, SC
20 August 2021